I KNOW
WHAT
TO DO,
SO WHY
DON'T
I DO IT?

I KNOW WHAT TO DO, SO WHY DON'T I DO IT?

MIND YOUR **EMOTIONS** TO END **PROCRASTINATION** AND **ACHIEVE** ALL YOUR GOALS

NICK HALL, PhD

Published 2022 by Gildan Media LLC
aka G&D Media
www.GandDmedia.com

FIRST EDITION 2022

Front Cover design by David Rheinhardt of Pyrographx

Interior design by Meghan Day Healey of Story Horse, LLC

Library of Congress Cataloging-in-Publication Data is available upon request

ISBN: 978-1-7225-0570-7

10   9   8   7   6   5   4   3   2   1

Contents

Introduction

Some undertakings, such as filing income tax returns are short-term tasks, while others exist as dreams tucked away on your bucket list for "someday." It seems the things we want to do get done, while those we need to do make their annual appearance as fleeting New Year's resolutions—remember the diet, daily walk, and plans to clean out the garage?

You're not alone.

What many of us share in common is a tendency to procrastinate. That applies to finishing this book! Indeed, there's good chance that despite your best intentions, you may not arrive at the last page, which is why I'm going to give you a quick-start guide right now to identify the all-important reward—that sometimes elusive carrot we all need to keep us chugging along. You'll need to delve into your past to learn how best to unlock your motivation.

Start by recalling a pursuit you undertook with ease. You had plenty of drive, overcame obstacles, and achieved your goal effortlessly. Perhaps you were on your high school swim team and looked forward to the alarm clock jarring you from a deep sleep so you could make the pre-dawn practice. Maybe it was the preparation required to excel on the school's debate team, or the weekends spent tinkering with your vintage car's engine so you could squeeze a little more horsepower from it.

If you completed a goal once, you can do it again. You just need to identify what it was that propelled you toward your goal. That's how I identified the key ingredient of my past success.

Lawrence Welk of champaign music fame along with the rock and roll teen idol, Bobby Vee were based in the Dakotas. That might explain why music ruled at my junior high school in South Dakota and I was all in. Whether it was the marching band, jazz band, or orchestra, I could be found coaxing melodies from my trumpet. My academic grades suffered terribly because those subjects bored me to tears. Instead of math and history, I scrutinized sheet music and practiced each evening and most weekends—classical music, jazz, and even repetitive scales. It was my passion, and I had no difficulty summoning the motivation to press my lips to the mouthpiece.

The Rapid City school system had an exceptional and extremely competitive music program. Once each month, band members could challenge the person in the chair ahead of them for the more prestigious spot. Steve Calhoun and I were constantly competing with each other for the coveted first-chair position, which we took turns occupying. Our fellow band members decided who was most deserving after appraising our solos. We were equals and the most capable musicians in the trumpet section. One of us was always in the top seat.

After a year in this environment, my family moved to Chicopee, Massachusetts, where the only music program was at the local high school. It would be another year before I would become a student there, however, I was invited to play in their band whenever I had time. I showed up for practice and learned the first chairs in all the sections were reserved for seniors regardless of their ability to perform. I played better than all of them, yet there was no way I could advance until several years later when I eventually reached my senior year. I walked out and never played again.

Years later while pondering why I didn't continue with an activity that gave me so much pleasure, I realized my motivation to play was fueled not so much by playing music, but by the competition—by the adrenaline rush while waiting to learn whether I would be bumped back or remain in first chair or wondering if I would flub a note during a concert. It was the nervous excitement that drove me.

That was more than sixty years ago, and during the interim, I've held a variety of jobs, some dangerous, and each with no guarantee of long-term employment. Upon reflection, every job I accepted was associated with a larger than usual amount of risk, and I enjoyed them all.

For me to start and finish a project requires that I find some way to incorporate an element of risk. If nothing else, I'll always find it at the eleventh hour while frantically racing the clock to finish on time. An excess of often unwarranted optimism didn't allow the prospect of failure to hold me back. Excitement is what I found rewarding.

I'm not telling you this because I think you thrive on excitement. Instead, I'm suggesting you apply the same process I did to identify the type of reward that will drive you to success. Reflect on what it was you found sufficiently rewarding so that you worked night and day to achieve a long ago objective. Chances are it's what you still find rewarding today. That's the component you need to weave into your endeavors. Use what you find rewarding to maintain your motivation even when faced with challenges.

If you get as far as chapter 3, you'll understand why identifying a reward is the key to breaking the procrastination cycle. If you don't make it that far, at the very least you've already learned the importance of identifying a reward even though you may not appreciate why. If you do get to the end of this book, you'll fully understand why you know what to do but why you won't do it.

At first glance, the answer to this question may seem straightforward: "Just do it!" Not so fast. As you begin to turn the pages, you'll quickly discover that, while easy to say, heeding Nike's advertising slogan is an entirely different matter. I'm sure you know this or else you wouldn't feel the need to read this book.

As you turn the pages, you'll realize procrastination is not due to haphazard time-management skills.

It stems from poor emotion management, as I'll explain in chapter 1. Let's face it, you'll have no problem finding the time to file a tax return when you're expecting a substantial refund. But the same amount of time will be spent doing all sorts of unimportant projects to delay filing when you think you'll have to send the IRS a check. Time is not the issue. You're procrastinating in order to postpone the distress experienced when you calculate how much you owe.

We perform tasks to satisfy a desire. The Nobel Prize laureate Bertrand Russell identified the common human desires as love of power, the acquisition of possessions, rivalry, and vanity. Secondary desires include knowledge, delight, and excitement. When a desire is satisfied, we experience pleasure, and when our quest to satisfy that desire is thwarted, we experience displeasure.

Cutting to the chase, we do (or don't do) things to experience pleasure or to avoid pain. It's the reason your boss wields a stick or carrot to ensure things get done. For me, the carrot is in the form of excitement, while the stick represents boredom.

So far so good. But life becomes complicated with the realization that the motivation to start or delay a task is a tug-of-war between positive and negative emotions. Who wants to tackle cleaning the toilet when you have the option of hanging out with friends? Or perhaps the work assignment you've been given stretches the limits of your skill set. Fear of failure begins to overshadow the anticipated pleasure associated with eventual success. Your motivation to continue is consumed. Motivation is not a skill. Like a muscle, it's subject to fatigue when stretched. Steps need to be taken to replenish it upon completing a long and arduous task.

This concept is explained in detail in chapters 2 and 3. While practical solutions are offered, more important is gaining an understanding of how choices are made. That understanding will enable you to customize the information to best suit your personality and values. One size never has nor will fit all when it comes to behavior, so your reasons for not achieving goals may differ markedly from those of your colleagues and friends.

This point is a central tenet of this book. View the options presented in the same way you would a restaurant menu; select those strategies that best fit your lifestyle, temperament, and personality.

Equally important for success is the need to remove obstacles. Failing to do so will result in your taking three steps forward while sliding back two. Progress will be painstakingly slow. Perhaps one of the greatest impediments you'll face is stress, which also can set the stage for other barriers to slow your progress. Unrelenting stress may erode your immune system and leave you vulnerable to infection. It makes sense. Achieving a goal is going to be tough when running a fever and dealing with a virus.

It's just as tough to achieve goals when you awaken exhausted after spending most of the night worrying about deadlines. Sleep can be disrupted for a number of reasons, including lots of hassles. Too often, sleep is regarded as the obligatory end of a day. It's viewed as a reserve of time by students pulling all-nighters while cramming for an exam. It's the metaphorical bank from which you borrow extra time to finish writing a report because you were careless with how you spent your minutes during the day.

Inadequate sleep can result in any number of progress-blocking consequences. That's why you should view sleep not as the end of the current day, but as the beginning of the next. You'll learn more about this topic and how to get energized in chapter 10.

Of course, you may not remember the information you crammed during the night, nor the information you need to complete a report. You'll fall short not because fear of failure is bouncing off the walls of your brain's emotion center, but because memory neurons in your brain also take a hit in the wake of unexpected setbacks.

There are many reasons/excuses we conjure to convince ourselves delaying is a reasonable option. Each chapter will focus on the primary categories of these excuses. For example, the roles played by beliefs and emotions. Those chapters will address the lack of motivation, and address the "why *won't* I do it?" component of the question. However, physical limitations cannot be ignored, which reveals the second component of the question, "why *can't* I do it?"

Neither is mutually exclusive because mental processes sapping your motivation can impact your physical health, while physical limitations can impact your will to proceed. That's why other chapters will address ways to optimize your immune system, obtain restful sleep, and include nutrients that can impact your mood. You'll also discover the value of social networks and strategies for dealing with difficult people who stand in your way.

Realize you are not alone. When you ask yourself why you don't start or complete important tasks, it's a question countless others have asked and with regrettable consequences. Perhaps an exceptionally talented artist who succumbed to self-doubt and never pursued their passion. A salesperson who lost an important contract when fear of failure prompted her to postpone the closure. A brilliant engineer who abandoned a revolutionary idea fearing ridicule and rejection.

Don't worry. You're in good company, but not for long if you apply the knowledge you're about to gain. That's because the purpose of this book is not just to answer the question, "I know what to do, so why don't I do it?" My primary intent is to provide you with the understanding and skills to avoid ever having to ask yourself that question again.

Obtaining that understanding will likely start you along a path leading to a more productive and fulfilling life. If you're like me, you won't embrace a solution merely because someone told you to. You want to know why a strategy is likely to work. Indeed, "Because it doesn't make sense" or "I don't understand why this is important" could have been chapter headings. Instead, I chose to dispatch these pretexts indirectly by providing you with the necessary knowledge to decide for yourself whether a particular strategy might be suited to your personality and temperament. Of course you should also establish the credibility of the information's source.

My interest in the subject of procrastination is both personal and academic. Personal because I've often posed the question that serves as the title of this book. Academic because I felt the answer involved more than merely tidying up my calendar, making lists, and setting priorities. It struck me that attributing a behavior as complex as procrastination to a single primary cause such as time management was inconsistent with the inner workings of the human brain.

My formal training began with an undergraduate degree in psychology, followed by a doctorate in neuroscience, which then was topped off with two years of postdoctoral training in immunology. For more than forty years I pursued a research career linking the three subjects into the field of psychoneuroimmunology.

I now apply that research helping corporate leaders and athletes deal with health and performance-destructive emotions related to stress and change. My academic background and work with clients have convinced me that human behavior and the brain that guides it are extremely complex.

I recall a poster stating that if the brain were simple enough for us to understand, we would be too stupid to understand it. How true! That's why my advice to clients is guided by a more integrated and holistic approach than is offered in many other self-improvement books.

If you're looking for a quick fix to launch you along a journey to success, you won't find it in the pages of this book. One size never has nor ever will fit all in biology and medicine, so even if I were to make a list of step-by-step solutions, they would work for only certain readers. My intent has been to provide a resource you can use to create your own formulas.

Each chapter delves into a rationale that begins with the word *because*. Some excuses may resonate with you more than others; however, like the human body and its parts, you should realize the subject of each chapter is inextricably related to all the others. Which ones are the primary origin of your procrastination will soon become apparent as you apply the information to your own circumstances.

It is my sincere hope that, upon finishing this book, you will know what to do along with an awareness of how to do it.

1

Because I Always Procrastinate

The Problem

The timing of your company's product launch is critical. If the new software is made available before testing is complete and then fails to meet the expectations of clients, it will be a severe blow to your organization's stellar reputation.

On the other hand, if the competition gets their version to market first, losing that edge will cost your company millions in lost sales. It's been more than a month since you accepted responsibility to compile a detailed analysis of current marketing trends along with other data essential to the decision-making process. Your report and recommendation are due in one week. But you haven't even started!

You may never have been in this predicament; however, we all have faced rapidly approaching deadlines after leaving tasks to the last minute.

As a student, you may have delayed preparing for a final exam or writing a paper. You may have left unsaid what needed saying to sustain a relationship. To this day, you deeply regret having missed a golden opportunity when you needlessly delayed making a decision. Yet again, you have canceled the cancer screening appointment.

Despite knowing what needed to be done, you simply didn't do it, perhaps using one of the following excuses to justify your decision:

- There aren't enough hours in the day.
- I've got other things I want to do first.
- Something unexpected came up.
- There's still plenty of time.
- I don't want to deal with the follow-up.
- Someone else can do it.

Time is the common thread binding many of the excuses we use to justify doing tomorrow what should and could be done today. It's also the dimension to which many people attribute their inability to complete tasks. It's the reason time management is embedded in the titles of countless books recommending an assortment of strategies to better utilize this most precious of all commodities. These strategies include lists, color coding, sticky notes, breaking complex tasks into more manageable components, and who knows what else.

While time management enables you to use your time more efficiently, it ignores the primary reason you miss deadlines: You don't start. Lacking the motivation to begin a task is the hallmark of procrastination.

Definition

Procrastination has two meanings: one derived from the Latin root meaning to delay until tomorrow, and the other from the Greek root meaning to do something counter to good judgment. Both involve motivation, which comes from the Latin root meaning to move.

While time management will enable you to use time more efficiently, it will not provide the motivation required to start. That's an emotion-management issue and, once successfully overcome, will allow access to a pathway that often can whisk you along to the finish in considerably less time than you anticipated. I've lost track of the number of times I've finished a long-delayed project much quicker than anticipated, only to be left wondering why I put it off for so long.

Many of my clients have commented that, once they start, everything comes together quickly and, somehow, they manage to meet what once was viewed as a seemingly impossible deadline. They justify their habit of waiting until the eleventh hour because, "I work best under pressure."

What they're really saying is they need a high level of motivation to begin. It may be their best, but it's certainly not the best they could do in the absence of the fatigue and anxiety characteristic of eleventh-hour efforts. They run on pure adrenaline, which enables them to burn the midnight oil and somehow sneak under the wire. In many situations, postponing the commencement of a project can be detrimental. However, there are circumstances when delaying the start of a project might be beneficial. Let me explain, next.

Procrastination or Reflection

For over twenty years, I depended on research grants to support my laboratories and personnel. There were many occasions when I didn't begin preparing a grant application until the deadline was dangerously close.

Instead, I was riding my bicycle on off-road trails or paddling my kayak on a local river. At first glance, this was a textbook example of procrastination. Far from it! I was thinking far away from distractions. At the time, only a handful of scientists believed the brain was capable of modulating the immune system, and even fewer thought there was any merit to searching for signals the immune system might be sending to the brain. Identifying those potential and elusive substances is what I struggled to convince the NIH was worthy of pursuit.

But how do you start writing an application to study something with very little data to support even a shakier hypothesis? A convincing argument will come together only after a considerable amount of thought and reflection.

Whether being engaged in thought processes constitutes procrastination is arguable. However, the fact remains taking time to reflect, even if it results in a delayed start, can culminate in highly beneficial outcomes. It was while working on my doctorate that I discovered the value of taking time to think. My adviser often chastised me for sailing in the Florida Keys with my wife over long weekends or disappearing for a week or more while my classmates were laboring in labs. But he never stopped me because he knew I was extremely productive when I was at work. Indeed, over the four years of training, I generated more publications than many of the students who never took a break.

When contemplating a perplexing problem, I'll often experience the elusive aha moment while immersed in nature. Indeed, I did this so much I habitually found myself completing urgent tasks minutes before the deadline or apologizing for being late. However, once I did start the grant writing process or experiment, the time spent outdoors enabled me to finish in much less time than I might have otherwise. It also may be the reason the task seemed easier after procrastinating. It may not be the deadline-related pressure, but the time spent reflecting that hastened the process. For me, it paid off.

Over several decades, I enjoyed a very productive research career. My scientific observations resulted in numerous publications that received national and international recognition. Once I collected sufficient data substantiating that the brain and immune system were linked, more and more grant money flowed into the lab. My success was due in large part to taking time to think and reflect.

On the surface, it could be argued I was procrastinating. However, my behavior was not an escape from the tedium of the grant writing process. Instead, it was an immersion in the planning phase, which couldn't evolve into the start of writing until I was satisfied the proposed research would be successful. There are other examples of discoveries made not while focused on the problem, but during periods of recovery and reflection.

In 1665, Christiaan Huygens was researching ways to improve the accuracy and durability of clocks so they could be used by mariners navigating the world's oceans. Being able to record the angle of the sun at precisely 12 noon GMT was critical for pinpointing their location. Then, his work was interrupted when an upper respiratory infection forced him to remain in bed away from his workshop. He whiled away the time observing pendulum clocks mounted on the wall of his bedroom. In doing so, he noticed that the clocks eventually became synchronized even after he deliberately altered the swing of their pendulums.

The principle of synchronicity arose from that chance observation. It was a milestone in physics that did not start out as a goal. It was the result of an astute observation, which would probably never have happened had Huygens's focus been elsewhere. The principle of synchronicity eventually was paramount centuries later during the development of superconductors and pacemakers.

He achieved success not by focusing on the details of a specific goal, but by being observant and recognizing clues in the periphery.

Similarly, Albert Einstein had a breakthrough moment, not while working through mathematical equations when seated at his desk, but while staring out to sea aboard the ship conveying him to the United States. Taking time to reflect should not be mistaken for procrastination, which entails deliberate avoidance.

An Emotion-Management Problem

Many of us have been taught that procrastination is synonymous with laziness. The recipient of this label is viewed as unreliable and even incompetent, not only by others, but as a self-assessment. We're aware we are intentionally avoiding the task at hand, which we know is wrong. However, rather than being a character flaw due to the inability to understand the concept of time, it's a strategy for coping with negative emotions.

- Perhaps you resent the fact you were stuck with the project instead of someone else.
- You find the task boring.
- You worry about lacking the skills to accomplish the task.
- Anxiety builds due to fear of failure.
- You're afraid of being labeled as unreliable or incompetent by others.

These thoughts are amplified by the Judeo-Christian work ethic commanding that adherents labor hard to achieve success and salvation. *Idle hands are the devil's workshop!* As a consequence, some people routinely delay starting important tasks until it becomes a habit. Even simple-to-do tasks are put off. When you move a time-sensitive task to a back burner, it may be out of sight, but I can assure you it's not out of mind. If it's a work-related project, you'll be surrounded at your desk with hard-to-ignore reminders especially as the due date looms closer.

These constant reminders, even at the subconscious level, will trigger a gradual increase in anxiety as you begin to reflect on the consequences of either not completing the project on time or rushing the process and then suffering in the aftermath for having produced an inferior product.

If you continue to postpone an important discussion that is necessary to resolve a conflict, your well-being will be impacted in a dual manner: (1) by prolonging the unresolved conflict and (2) suffering the impact saying what needs to be said may have on the overall relationship. In both settings, you'll feel inadequate, especially if you compare yourself with others who cheerfully meet deadlines and have the confidence to resolve issues before they get out of hand.

How ironic that what we think is escaping stress is actually creating more. This, in turn, further reduces the level of motivation you need to get started.

Getting Started

Nike's clever marketing slogan, Just Do It, increased shoe sales, but the suggestion won't help you break the inertia impeding the start of an important project. That's because willpower is not a skill you can finely hone through practice and elicit on demand. Instead, willpower has many similarities with a muscle in that it can wear down and tire after excessive use. Research has shown that the more motivation required to achieve a goal, the less willpower you'll have available in the immediate aftermath. I've observed this as both a scientist and teacher.

Before heading to graduate school, I was part of a team studying communication patterns in bottlenose dolphins for the Office of Naval Research. (Flipper of TV fame was a charming bottlenose dolphin.)

I was chosen for this job because of my summer job wrestling alligators at the Black Hills Reptile Gardens in South Dakota. The US Navy figured anyone who could handle large alligators could handle dolphins. Because of my undergraduate training in experimental psychology, my job was to train the dolphins to recognize different types of communication signals emitted by other dolphins. It involved starting with freshly captured dolphins and training them to press an underwater paddle, but only upon hearing a very specific vocalization. The animal was to ignore all others.

It took several long days, some stretching into the night, to teach the animals what was expected in order to receive a reward of fish. During that time, the animals worked hard and expressed frustration when mistakes were made. But once they figured out what had to be done, the training sessions had to end. The animals had used up all their willpower trying different approaches until they achieved the goal of pressing the paddle only when they detected a specific sound from among the large number being transmitted through the underwater speaker. They had reached what experimental psychologists call a plateau, which is the interval before they can arouse sufficient motivation to continue.

You may have experienced such a plateau as a student. Following a major exam, you were likely drained. The next day you had to force yourself to open the textbook and resume studies. Most likely, you took a day or two off. After expending a large amount of time, perhaps several weeks learning the material before you eventually received the reward (the end of the exam), you were done. It might have been several days before you began the assigned readings. It's why, as a teacher, I always made it a point to administer important exams during the last class period of the week, so students had the weekend to replenish their motivation.

My work with dolphins taught me there was no point introducing new and sometimes difficult concepts in the wake of a hard-earned reward. Other research has shown the length of the plateau is proportional to the amount of effort required to achieve the goal. That's consistent with Isaac Newton's observation that for every action, there will be an equal and opposite reaction. Clear off for a long weekend. Party as though there'll be no tomorrow. In other words, study hard then play just as hard. You need to apply this concept to yourself and to others when undertaking or assigning a task.

In the context of dealing with procrastination, make sure you don't attempt to begin a lengthy and involved project soon after or while engaged in another task of equal complexity. Examples of motivation-draining projects might include

- Days spent planning a dinner party using a new and tricky recipe for more than a dozen guests
- Comparing the education options during the weeks leading up to your child's first day of school
- Going through a messy divorce
- Buying a house
- Recovering from a long illness
- Making wedding preparations

These are just a few examples of motivation-sapping events. If you can, avoid accepting responsibility to take on another demanding task until at least a few days have passed. If you happen to be the person assigning tasks, keep this in mind when selecting a person or team to undertake a project. Some emotions will activate brain circuits that hinder the pursuit of a goal. They are referred to as negative emotions and induce avoidance or withdrawal behaviors.

That's the last thing you want to deal with when trying to start work on a complicated project. In addition, emotions continue to play a role throughout the process. During the pursuit of a goal, events that slow progress can give way to anger, while an unexpected opportunity that hastens progress can bring about joy.

Thus, emotions provide the motivation to achieve a goal, with new ones arising during the pursuit. At both the start and during the process, emotions are driving or moving our behavior. That's why your ability to manage emotions is paramount to your overcoming procrastination. It doesn't matter whether you're attempting to quit smoking or launching a fundraiser for the PTA. Successful management of emotions requires an understanding of what they are, where they come from, and what they can do.

Takeaways

- Procrastination is delaying the start of an undertaking.
- Failing to finish a task is an emotion-management problem, not a time-management problem.
- Motivation resembles a muscle in that it needs time to recover.
- Don't confuse procrastination with taking time to reflect and plan.
- A demanding task in your personal life can temporarily lower your motivation to undertake projects at work.
- Balance the expenditure of motivation with an interval of recovery.

2

Because I'm Too Emotional

Emotions play a key role during the achievement of goals, especially when summoning the motivation to being. Indeed, the word *motivation* shares the same underlying Latin root with *motivate*, which means to move. Emotions also serve as the link between your beliefs and how you conduct your life.

In addition, emotions can impact your immune system and memory as well as your cardiovascular and endocrine systems. Even your reaction time and ability to perform can be influenced by emotions. In fact, there's hardly any behavior or bodily function that remains free from their influence.

Realize that all emotions, however, even those regarded as negative, serve an important purpose. For instance, sadness can distract you from making progress, or it can prompt you to change your circumstances. Fear may stop you in your tracks, or it can motivate you to take precautionary steps. Without emotions, your life would be dull and meaningless. But too much of a good thing at the wrong time can also derail you.

What Are Emotions?

First and foremost, you should recognize that emotions are really nothing more than a sensory system. They are the eyes and ears of your body—gauges of your biology. More often than not, negative emotions reflect the perception of unmet needs. A predicament may give rise to anger or fear. But it's important to realize that emotion itself is not the problem. Instead, the emotion is a response to what gave rise to it. Furthermore, problems result only when the emotion or the manner in which it's expressed is not warranted.

Many people make the mistake of believing the emotion is the problem. They purchase a book proclaiming to have the solution for vanquishing their anger and reducing their fear. That's all well and good. By all means, take steps to counter the fear of failure impeding your productivity. However, recognize that if all you do is place a pharmacologic or behavioral Band-Aid on the emotion, the problem that led to that emotion will resurface at some future time. It might be in the form of a derailed immune system, intestinal upset, skin disease, memory loss, or heart problems.

Any one of the resultant symptoms will impede making progress toward a goal independent of motivation. Indeed, a large number of illnesses will more readily occur when your body has been altered by emotional upheaval. When that happens, you have the answer to the question: I know what to do, so why *can't* I do it?

There are over 500 words in just the English language with emotional connotations. Some people consider each of these words to be an individual emotion. Of course, that gets a bit unwieldy. In contrast, the British philosopher John Locke argued that there are only two emotions: those giving rise to pain and those resulting in pleasure. Negative emotions are those associated with a threat or with the thwarting of a goal, while positive emotions are associated with pleasure or with making progress toward a goal.

Is it that simple? Are emotions just good or bad? History tells us the answer is no.

Greek philosophers might have argued that all emotions are good. That the ability to express all the emotions is essential to experience the good life. A counterpoint was promoted by the Stoics who argued it was a waste of time to experience emotions, especially joy and love, which were considered frivolous. You can't blame them. Life was absolutely chaotic during that era in Roman history, devoid of many things that give rise to pleasure or joy.

The belief that emotions are inherently bad was driven home during the Middle Ages. What today we would call emotion was, during that church-dominated period of history, closely intertwined with sin. Words such as *greed*, *lust*, and *envy* were in the spotlight. To this day, this historical perspective influences our cultural beliefs. Despite evidence to the contrary, emotions often are believed to be inherently bad, which may be why many people deny or repress them.

You've heard the expressions or perhaps used them yourself: Don't be so emotional. Chill out. Be more reasonable. The implication is that emotions are the opposite of reason and that if you express your feeling, you have lost control. This cultural belief may well explain the reluctance, especially by men in Western society, to express their feelings.

Pain versus Pleasure

People do things primarily for one of two reasons: to avoid discomfort or to experience pleasure. If a child has a traumatic experience as a result of being punished for expressing anger, she will associate anger with discomfort and will avoid expressing it. If a boy is brought up in an environment where he is taught a man should be strong and in charge, he will likely avoid the expression of fear. As a consequence, both the emotion and the circumstances that might give rise to it are avoided.

The choice doesn't end here. If you are uncomfortable with the expression of a certain emotion, you may very well align yourself with an individual who also feels uncomfortable expressing the same emotion. Whether in the workplace or the family, you reinforce each other and behave in a way you both are comfortable with by avoiding the same emotion.

In the context of tackling important undertakings, the key is to associate as many positive features as possible with either the project or its completion. If you reflect on your past accomplishments, you undoubtedly had no difficulty doing what you wanted to do: planning a vacation, working on your hobby, shopping, or going out to dinner, for example. The problem is not a matter of malaise and not wanting to do anything; the challenge is prioritizing what needs to be done over what you want to do.

If you derive pleasure from a large number of endeavors, then chances are the more you will procrastinate because you'll likely have more positive options to choose from than those you find onerous.

All Emotions Are Both Positive and Negative

Over the years, many ways of categorizing emotions have been proposed. However, from the standpoint of understanding their role when setting about to begin a task, the simplest grouping is best. Accordingly, emotions can be viewed as being either positive or negative. Positive ones such as love and joy will motivate you to engage in approach behaviors, while negative ones, such as fear and sadness, will motivate you to engage in avoidance behavior. We seek more of what provides pleasure and less of what causes pain. Hence, emotions prompt us to move to or from the circumstances triggering it.

I was once asked to present a lecture entitled The Power of Positive Emotions. It was only a thirty-minute talk, but I spent more time working on that short lecture than I often expend when designing a multi-day program for a large corporation. There were two reasons for this: the person presenting before me was Richard Simmons, and the person coming on stage immediately after was Naomi Judd.

I was well aware that nobody really cared about me. Most probably the audience members had no idea who I was and little interest in what I had to say. I had been hired by the organizers to bridge the gap between the lighthearted, fun presentation of diet guru Simmons, cavorting about the stage in his pink and white shorts and tank top, and the very serious, spiritual message of Naomi Judd. The organizers estimated it would take about thirty minutes to change the set, so my job was to keep the audience occupied in the meantime.

Actually, knowing I was a placeholder and not the main event was not the problem. Indeed, it was a challenge I enjoyed facing. The difficulty was deciding which emotions belonged in the positive column and which in the negative one. I couldn't decide. Oh, I read the same books you've probably read, but I couldn't agree with the authors.

And then one morning when I was out riding my bicycle, I experienced an aha moment (during the type of reflection time I explained in the previous chapter). It finally dawned on me that there is no such thing as a positive emotion. All emotions are negative. At the same time, I also concluded there are no negative emotions. They are all positive. It is not the emotion that is positive or negative. It is the context in which it arises. It is the match or mismatch between the emotion and the circumstance that determines whether the same emotion can be positive or negative. Let's consider a couple of examples.

Anger is often placed in the negative column, which it most certainly can be. For example, when your pent-up anger is taken home from work and then misdirected at your children or spouse (or kicking the dog is one descriptor) instead of the coworker or supervisor who has wronged you, it most certainly does belong in the negative column. But if you use anger as a source of motivation to identify to others the underlying problem and then express it in an appropriate way, it belongs in the positive column. Thus, anger can be either a virtue or a vice.

Conversely, the emotion of love is routinely placed in the positive column, especially when directed at your children, parents, or your spouse. But when that same emotion of love is directed at the spouse of your neighbor, it can be a destructive emotion. So is the expression of love depicted in many Valentine's Day cards. The ones proclaiming, "I couldn't live without you." "I love you so much my life would not be complete if you were not a part of it." This, I believe, is a sick, codependent form of love, which stifles independence and the opportunity to grow.

If you delve into history and literature, you discover that what happened to Romeo and Juliet was the rule, not the exception. That kind of dependent love gets people imprisoned in castles, run over by trains, or murdered. Of course that's assuming they don't commit suicide first.

The same is true of beliefs. There is no such thing as a good or bad belief. It's only when a belief is not justified under a particular set of circumstances that it becomes bad. Like the emotions they can give rise to, it is the match between a belief and the circumstances that has to be examined.

Even though beliefs and emotions are distinct entities, be aware that beliefs give rise to emotions, which activate chemicals capable of impacting your entire body. Thus, when you change a belief, it will most likely evoke, via emotions, changes in both your mental and physical health.

When the Blues Set In

At various times, we all experience what is usually described as the blues. When present, it's difficult, if not impossible, to do what you know you should. The treatment of these minor, sub-clinical depressions should focus initially on determining to what degree environmental factors are responsible for the symptoms. While the blues can progress to major clinical depression, there are vast differences between these two conditions. Clinical or major depressions are generally defined as those due to biochemical disturbances within the brain.

A number of psychological disorders can be directly linked with chronic stress, although depression is one of the more common consequences. Up to 10 percent of the population will experience a major depression at some point during their lives. There also are different forms of depression.

Reactive depression is a response to something that is readily apparent, such as the loss of a job or the loss of a loved one. Sometimes depression may be caused by factors that aren't readily apparent. An example is bipolar depression, which is characterized by negative emotions alternating with periods of mania. There is also schizo-affective disorder, which is characterized by episodes of schizophrenia interspersed with depression.

Major depression can be recognized through several unrelenting symptoms, including these:

- Overwhelming fatigue
- Impaired concentration
- Impaired memory
- Feelings of worthlessness
- Feeling overwhelmed
- Increase or decrease in appetite
- Changes in sleep behavior
- Decreased ability to experience pleasure

A change in diet, regular exercise, and psychotherapy can each help in alleviating the symptoms of depression. But before embarking on a course of self-prescribed remedies, it is important to seek professional medical advice to first rule out the presence of serious illness.

Counseling can be helpful for individuals suffering from an array of emotional difficulties. Individuals suffering from depression, anxiety, relationship problems, eating disorders, panic attacks, phobias, or addictions may benefit from treatments offered by mental health professionals.

In addition, therapy can be of great benefit in dealing with stressful events and major life transitions. These may include job or relationship loss, parenting issues, as well as stress-related illnesses. Therapy can often help people adjust more quickly and effectively to adverse events.

If professional help is not warranted, the next section offers some steps you can take to minimize the impact these symptoms might have upon your doing the things you should be undertaking.

Ways to Deal with Emotional Turmoil

Translate your emotions into language. Talk out loud or simply write about the event(s) giving rise to the emotion. This will enable you to evaluate the problem via a different sensory modality, thereby providing a different perspective from which to identify potential solutions.

Identify the emotion you are experiencing. Are you feeling sad, angry, fearful, guilty, embarrassed, or a combination of these or others? Next, identify the source of the emotion. Are you angry with yourself for not accomplishing a goal? Are you fearful or sad about the consequences? Are you feeling guilty because you failed?

At this point, evaluate your reaction from a realistic perspective. You'll likely realize that some of your thoughts are grossly exaggerated, in which case replace them with more rational thoughts. For example, if you happen to be late for a meeting, don't assume your coworkers will think you are irresponsible. Recognize that they will probably accept that your tardiness was due to reasons outside your control.

As a result of going through these simple steps, you probably have already avoided an emotion-fueled crisis. When you determine what went wrong, take corrective action. Learn from your mistakes and set about to keep emotions from preventing you from getting things done again.

About that presentation I made after Richard Simmons and before Naomi Judd, I think it went well. At least the audience remained seated and didn't boo me off the stage, which is one of my measures of success.

Takeaways

- The root of the word *emotion* is to move.
- Emotions motivate you to meet unmet needs.
- Positive emotions are associated with approach while negative emotions are associated with avoidance.
- All emotions have the potential to be negative when expressed inappropriately.
- When emotions cannot be managed, professional help should be sought.
- Transforming emotions into words can reveal solutions for better managing them.

3

Because I'm Afraid I'll Fail

Of all the emotions, fear of failure is the primary basis of procrastination. However, seldom does an emotion exist in isolation. For example, fear and anger often are displayed together. Throw sadness and regret into the mix and lessening their combined impact upon motivation becomes all the more challenging. The following experience illustrates the way emotions and motivation go hand in hand.

Stranger in a Foreign Land

At the age of ten, I arrived in the United States from England excited to be in a foreign country, but sad knowing friends and familiar surroundings were thousands of miles away. Adjusting to school was particularly challenging. I was a newcomer attempting to be accepted into long-established cliques. Despite speaking English,

I didn't speak with the pronounced American accent that characterized the speech patterns of my peers.

Ridicule and taunting began when I walked into class wearing my former English school uniform (blazer and neck tie accompanied with color coordinated shorts and knee socks). It continued when the teacher announced it was time for a restroom break. I had no idea what he was referring to. Had he said toilet, loo, or lavatory, I would have understood. But restroom? I had no idea where we were going and didn't want to show my ignorance by asking. So I pondered the word trying to guess what it was. All I could think of was restaurant, especially since it was late morning and a reasonable time for lunch. Imagine my embarrassment when I was the only kid standing in front of a urinal holding a sandwich!

Sadness stemming from being away from friends, fear resulting from not knowing what embarrassing situation I'd find myself in next, along with anger that I had no say in moving to this strange new country formed the ingredients in the potpourri of emotions I was experiencing. I had two choices: (1) avoid the negative emotions by escaping the school environment, perhaps by feigning illness, or (2) change the things I could and accept the things I couldn't. I picked option #2, which actually made things worse before they got better.

In preparation for my move across the Atlantic, my grandmother gave me copies of Mark Twain's *The Adventures of Tom Sawyer* and Harriet Beecher Stowe's *Uncle Tom's Cabin*. I read them both before departing thereby familiarizing myself with Americans living in nineteenth-century America, not those living a hundred years later. That realization prompted me to seek a more modern guide.

I'd never seen comic books in England; however, they were all the rage among my American schoolmates in 1958. I chose them as my guide to becoming Americanized. Through them, I learned the vernacular. However, my pronunciation of certain words led to even more embarrassment along with trouble.

"Hi, buster" was the comic-book-inspired greeting I used when encountering my classmates one Monday morning.

"What did you call me?" a classmate angrily demanded.

When I repeated what I thought was an acceptable greeting, he loudly informed the teacher, "Nicholas called me a bad word!"

I was ceremoniously kicked out of class and sent to the principal's office. Frustrated, I asked him how a word printed in a popular comic book and one I had heard others use could possibly be considered bad! He then asked me to spell the word I had used.

All was forgiven when he realized I had intended to say *buster*, which he and others heard with my enunciation as *bastard*. That's when I added "change my pronunciation of words" to my growing to-do list.

Those emotions I experienced soon after arriving in America drove my behavior. Without the frustration, sadness, and fear of being ostracized, I would have lacked the motivation to change.

Emotion Interference

It's not uncommon to experience conflicting emotions. When I'm conducting workshops with the objective of teaching the audience ways to make emotions work for instead of against them, I have them engage in a simple task that illustrates how emotions have the ability to cancel each other. You can try this with friends or colleagues and experience it yourself.

Instruct the participants to place the open palm of their right hand in front of the person to their right. Then have them place their left thumb against the outstretched palm of the person to their left. It works best when all are seated at a round table.

Explain how, upon hearing a particular word, they are to grab the thumb of the person seated to their right, while simultaneously avoid having their left thumb captured by the person to their left. Since many of my trainings deal with *stress*, that's the word I use. My routine is to start talking, then unexpectedly I'll shout the word *stress*. I'll do it a couple of times, occasionally throwing them off by substituting *dress* or *mess*. Very few people are successful in both trapping their neighbor's thumb while avoiding capture of their own.

Why? Because of what I call emotion interference. It's based on a principle in physics called destructive interference whereby two wave forms overlap and thus displace or cancel each other. It applies to many wave forms including sound. A car muffler uses this principle to displace sound waves generated by the engine, thereby significantly reducing the volume. A gun silencer utilizes the same principle.

Metaphorically, destructive interference is what happens in the brain when a person is asked to grab the thumb (approach) while simultaneously keeping their own from being trapped (avoidance).

Let's now apply this principle to emotions. Happiness motivates a person to approach more of what's bringing about this pleasant emotion, while sadness motivates avoidance of its triggers. The net result is they cancel each other out making it difficult if not impossible to be happy and sad at the same time. Here's an example of the same principle, but in the context of opposing emotions canceling out the motivation to avoid serious injury.

I'd taken over the alligator wrestling duties at the Reptile Gardens after the person doing that job suffered a severe bite injury. That should have been my first clue about the real dangers of this job. As the days passed without incurring any serious injuries, I became overly confident. In order to impress the large audience, I decided to take on the reptile that had incapacitated my predecessor. But I was no match for this large and aggressive beast. Twice, after I dragged it from the pool to the sand, it snapped its jaws and slapped me with its tail as it retreated to the water. The creature was heavy, and after three unsuccessful attempts, I realized if I didn't soon succeed, I'd be too tired to finish the show.

While pondering my options, I recalled having seen a member of the Seminole Indian tribe use a technique I had never attempted, but which would make it more difficult for the alligator to escape. It required my holding it by the tail, then jumping on its back from behind. It was on-the-job training as I made my move, landed on his back, then pressed down on his head to stop it from shaking.

Next I had to slide my hands alongside his jaws. As I grabbed his mouth and held his jaws closed with my left hand, a sharp pain enveloped my right hand. In my misguided attempt to show off and impress the audience, I had made a critical error.

In the same split second I grabbed his mouth with one hand, he clamped his teeth on the other. There I was sitting on an angry alligator holding his mouth closed with one hand with part of my other hand trapped between his sharp teeth. It was a real-life version of the parlor game I use in the team-building exercises and a metaphor for how emotion-induced behaviors can be negated by other emotions.

The dilemma I faced was having to let go of his jaw with one hand so he could open his mouth, thereby allowing me to extract my other hand. One hand wanted to escape, while the other instinctively held on. Approach versus avoidance. However, there was no guarantee if I let go that he would do the same.

My hand could be ripped off if he raced to the water without first letting me go. Two emotions were at play. In me, because I didn't know what the alligator was feeling. Fear, which had me in a near total state of withdrawal resulting in my sitting there doing nothing, and self-directed anger for (unlike the alligator) biting off more than I could chew.

Eventually, I gambled the alligator wanted to be rid of me as much as I wanted to be away from him. I let go, got off his back, and he followed suit. Then I slowly moved away breathing a long sigh of relief when he did the same. It's as though we implemented a carefully negotiated truce.

I'm fully aware the example I just gave is probably not one you or, for that matter, anyone with a lick of sense can readily relate to. Nonetheless, it's a metaphor for how emotions can interact. Fear cancels joy. If fear is present, the ability of a reward to deliver pleasure will be dramatically curtailed if not eliminated.

This concept is important to understand before agreeing to undertake a task as well as to whom you will delegate the responsibility should you find yourself in a supervisory role. That's because fear not only will moderate your response to the circumstances that resulted in the emotion, but other responses as well. Here are some examples of situations often associated with fear and anxiety—two emotions that can readily spill into other work and personal arenas.

- Your teenager has been injured in a car crash.
- Your partner has filed for divorce.
- You've been diagnosed with cancer.
- Your only child is heading off to college.
- You've been targeted by identity thieves.
- Your car needs expensive repairs you can't afford.

These are just a few life events capable of eliciting fear. For that matter, just about any event with unpredictable consequences and outside your control could be added to the list.

If you are experiencing any of these or other anxiety-causing circumstances, avoid accepting a key role on an important project. Wait until the stress abates. The same applies to delegating responsibility to others. Otherwise, the tendency to withdraw will only compound your tendency to procrastinate—itself a form of withdrawal. In other words, take your hand away from holding the alligator's mouth closed so you can get your other hand released from his jaws.

Let's be realistic. Many jobs do not allow the option of picking and choosing what and when you carry out an assignment. However, just an awareness of how your performance may be adversely affected will make it easier to adopt strategies to overcome the inertia preventing the start of an undertaking. You'll spend less time beating yourself up because you think you're lazy with the realization that external factors you can't control are partially to blame.

It's what Martin Seligman described as the optimistic explanatory style in his book, *Learned Optimism: How to Change Your Mind and Your Life*. Improved health and success are often correlated with people possessing this style. You won't cause the disruptive emotion to disappear; however, it will be easier to manage.

Losses Loom Greater Than Gains

There's a way you can change fear that works against you into an emotion that works to your advantage. You can actually transform inertia into action by converting fear of failure into fear of regret. Let me explain.

Research conducted by economists has revealed that people experience a greater amount of sadness following loss than the amount of pleasure experienced following a comparable gain. For example, if you found a $20 bill on the sidewalk, your good fortune would result in pleasure. On a scale of 1 to 10, you might experience pleasure at the level of 6. However, if that same $20 bill unknowingly fell from your pocket, your level of disappointment might register a 10 on a comparable scale. In other words, you would feel measurably worse about losing a twenty than if you found one.

Much of this research has been conducted in the context of predicting investors' choices when faced with a loss or gain in the value of their stocks. However, it applies to all behavior, including those associated with procrastination.

It's well recognized that emotions prevail over mathematically based analyses when predicting human behavior and the choices we make. Shift your focus from fear of failure if you take action to fear of regret if you don't. Take advantage of the extra momentum you'll achieve by viewing the outcome of your decision from the perspective of what you will lose (like a $20 bill, worse) instead of what you might gain (like a $20 bill, happy).

While in a weeklong kayak race around the state of Michigan, I was unable to avoid a bad storm and capsized in gale force winds and heavy seas. The mast of a small sail I relied on snapped in two, and my rudder broke. It was approaching midnight, and I was drifting in the growing swells of Lake Michigan a mile or so off a desolate section of coast. I used my VHF radio to summon the Coast Guard who came to my rescue.

On the way to their base, I lamented the damage and lost gear. It meant I wasn't going to finish. Sponsors would turn me down the next time I asked for support, and while my friends would be sympathetic, I knew they'd be disappointed. DNF (did not finish) would be etched next to my name in the official record. There were just too many reasons why I shouldn't try to continue. Those thoughts continued as I drifted off to sleep.

But early the next morning while resting in my hammock, I posed a different question: what would I regret if I dropped out without at least trying to get back under way? It was as though my rested state the next morning allowed me to recognize potential solutions with the same clarity as the rising sun illuminated my surroundings.

A Coast Guardsman gave me a ride to a local hardware store where I got supplies, then let me use the base workshop to fashion a makeshift mast and rudder. It was late in the afternoon when the storm finally subsided, and the lake settled down. By then the repairs were finished, my lost gear replaced, and I was ready to resume the race.

I changed fear of failure into fear of regret in not finishing, and that realization transformed my initial avoidance (desire to drop out) into approach (desire to press on). When I reached the finish, I learned I had won, not because I was the fastest contestant, but because the others dropped out when the storm hit! No one else in my boat category was left.

Fear of Failure

Procrastination is an avoidance behavior usually triggered by fear. It may be a complex task composed of multiple stages, each a large undertaking. If so, fear of failure may be driving your inability to start. It may be a straightforward task, but one requiring skills you think you lack.

Perhaps you underestimated the amount of time required when you agreed to take on a project. Some people have a strong need for social desirability and to be liked. They will say yes when they really wanted to say no and then realize they don't have time to deliver what they promised. Another possibility is recent events have sapped their motivation to do much of anything.

Scientists used to think motivation was a skill and if a person lacked it, it was a matter of plastering the wall with posters conveying affirming slogans or quotes to inspire them to take action. You've seen those missives in breakrooms and on office walls, people climbing mountains, rowing together, proclaiming the power of teamwork. It's now understood that motivation or willpower can be eroded by avoidance-triggering emotions such as fear.

If the childhood game rock-paper-scissors were about emotions, fear would always prevail. Fear would be the equivalent of rock to scissors, paper to rock, and scissors to paper. The reason this powerful emotion overshadows others is to optimize your survival. Better to waste a little biological energy fearing something that doesn't happen than to ignore a warning about something that does.

Experts have proposed many reasons explaining why so many of us procrastinate, but the primary one is fear. You may experience fear of failure stemming from self-doubt, or in the form of anxiety over missing a deadline. Ironically, you put off starting a project to avoid unpleasantness, yet the act of delaying brings on even more unpleasantness.

Much will depend on the nature of the task. For example, patrolling the lawn with a shovel in search of your dog's deposits is most unpleasant as would be scrubbing filthy floors. Instead, you busy yourself searching for online reviews of the new car you're thinking about buying or what you'll wear to your friend's wedding.

You'd think substituting a more enjoyable task for an unpleasant one would result in a stress-free respite. Actually, the opposite occurs because sensory cues in the environment will still be associated with the negative aspects of the task you're putting off. You still need to pick up dog poop.

Even at the subconscious level, avoidance will be enough to keep your neurons at the threshold of stress and anxiety. In addition, there are emotions associated with low self-esteem and self-blame, part of what are referred to as procrastinatory cognitions. Research has shown that these thoughts can significantly increase your levels of stress, which in turn can result in more fear-triggering procrastination. However, there is a way you can lessen the intensity of this emotion, thereby reducing its impact on your productivity. Let me explain.

Know More, Fear Less

Fear is the emotion of the future. If a dreaded event has come and gone, you no longer can be afraid of it. You can be angry, sad, even disgusted, but not afraid. The following is an example of how this emotion arises.

Mary has a fear of heights and is dreading the family's planned visit to the Grand Canyon. She's losing sleep worrying about getting close to the edge. When her husband and children set out, she tells them to go without her. Instead, she'll follow a marked trail well away from the edge of the canyon using a park brochure to identify the plants and wildlife along the way. They'll meet up later. It's a good solution with everyone doing what they enjoy.

That is, until Mary takes a wrong path leading to the edge of the precipice. She's no longer afraid of being at the edge because it's already happened. Now she's afraid of falling. At that moment, her husband and children unexpectedly arrive. Their calling out startles her as she begins to fall. She's no longer afraid of falling because it's already happening. Now she's afraid of landing!

This fictitious account is admittedly trite; however, it serves to illustrate how fear is associated not with the past or present, but with the future. Since the inability to predict drives fear, then the logical solution is to peer into the future to learn what happens next. Unfortunately, crystal balls exist only in the imagination of fiction writers, not the world we live in. But we can offset a lot of uncertainty through knowledge.

Collecting information is what I do when training and preparing for cross-country cycling trips. I've been riding bicycles across and up and down the United States since I was seventeen. During a five-year span starting in 2015, I covered over 10,000 miles raising money for Rotary International's End Polio campaign. Those journeys have been unsupported and have taken me from Oceanside, California, to St. Augustine, Florida, from my home in Tampa, Florida, to Toronto, Canada, and from Seattle, Washington, to Tampa.

It's a given that people I meet along the way will ask if I'm afraid of being hit by trucks or encountering bad weather. I tell them that while mindful of these risks, I'm not overly afraid. That's because over the course of more than fifty years, I've learned it's best to take measures to avoid dangerous situations than to exert my right of way. I also spend almost as much time researching the trips as I do training. It helps me predict.

Months before setting out, I'll contact the departments of transportation in the states I'll be passing through so I can familiarize myself with their bicycle regulations. States such as Texas and Montana allow cyclists to ride on the shoulder of interstate highways. Not all states are so accommodating so I check in advance before planning my route. I'll also contact bicycle shops seeking advice about local conditions, and review weather trends in recent years so I'm aware of temperature ranges and prevailing winds. I also carry a supply of spare tubes and parts so it's unlikely I'll be stranded. With a tent and sleeping bag, I never have to worry about where I'll spend the night because there's always the side of the road.

Most importantly, more than fifty years' experience has familiarized me with most any situation I might encounter. Of course there are always unexpected challenges, but that's what makes each journey an adventure and provides the inspiration to keep riding. Yes, my heart skipped a beat when a car mirror brushed my arm, and when I hurriedly sought shelter as a dust storm bore down on me in West Texas. But none of those or other close calls was sufficient to prompt me to stop riding.

My ability to predict has been sufficient to fend off fear, but not so absolute it instills boredom. Gather as much information as you can about the project details and potential obstacles. They won't magically disappear, but you'll be able to better apportion your time, and when progress is interrupted, your anxiety will be attenuated because your planning enabled you to anticipate the setback.

Overcoming Fear

It's now time to learn some skills to help you better handle fear. Many people cling to outmoded beliefs because they enable them to avoid an emotion that causes pain or discomfort. For example, complaining gets you nowhere. Let's imagine that this belief has its roots in early childhood when a complaint triggered a belligerent reaction on the part of a parent.

For example, let's say your dad believed children should be seen and not heard. Yes, in that environment and at that time, your behavior to keep your mouth shut was justified. It kept you out of trouble in the home. The fear response elicited by your parent's angry outburst had definite survival value. But things have changed now you're an adult.

In the retail store, it's not healthy to internalize anger because you still believe it's wrong to complain about having been overcharged. Or to fume about the overcooked steak and say nothing to the server. All you've done is replace the fear associated with speaking out with anger. Simply registering a complaint could so easily have dissipated that anger.

There are many things that you probably regret not having done out of fear. Even within the past twenty-four hours, you may well have stretched "turn the other cheek" beyond its intended boundary. Why? Probably because you wanted to avoid the fear that might have been precipitated had the other person responded like the adult in your life did so many decades ago.

The first question to ask is this: Is this belief that it's wrong to complain justified? The answer is no. There's nothing noble about being wronged and saying nothing. When you have been overcharged for a purchase, the belief that it is wrong to speak up is not justified.

Ask yourself: Is the belief serving a useful purpose? Of course not. It's serving a harmful purpose. Doing nothing is a behavior associated with a feeling of helplessness, which will erode your emotional well-being faster than almost anything else.

So what does all this have to do with procrastination and failing to do what you know you should? Everything.

Emotions tend to spill over and cause collateral damage to other aspects of your life. Fear-induced withdrawal triggered by an incident in your personal life will most assuredly accompany you into the workplace. Chances are, you'll be able to compartmentalize the matter and still make progress toward achieving your goals. However, that progress will be less efficient than it would have been without the distraction. You may think things are under control, but emotions tend to be disruptive even when they lurk below the conscious radar. Yet with practice you can gain greater control over your emotions.

Beginning today, practice dealing with change and the emotion of fear. For the next week, do one thing each day that is a departure from your normal way of behaving. It doesn't matter what it is. The only objective is to familiarize yourself with the feeling. And I'm not suggesting that you take up a dangerous sport or throw yourself in harm's way. You can do many activities that are quite safe from a physical standpoint, but that provide the opportunity to expand your emotional horizons.

For example, do you have a fear of public speaking? Then attend a PTA or city council meeting and make it a point to stand up and comment about an issue. Do the same at your next company training session. Ultimately, you might volunteer to make a presentation at a fund-raiser.

Are you overly competitive? Even on the highway, where you always want to be in front of the car ahead? Or first off the line at the traffic light? Then ease off on the accelerator and be a follower. Let another motorist move ahead so you can experience the emotion you have been trying to avoid. Indeed, it can be therapeutic to stop letting others influence your behavior by doing things on your terms.

Are you always in control and the expert in your organization? Then become a volunteer. Spend some time at a homeless shelter serving food or sweeping floors. Offer to help do something, knowing in advance that you have limited skills in this endeavor. Step out of your comfort zone and learn to accept advice and instruction from others.

I once enrolled in a five-day training program on how to run a ropes course. It was a new experience for me. For years, I'd been the person in front of the auditorium facilitating the training and answering questions. Suddenly, I found myself immersed in a group of people half my age and with largely physical education backgrounds instead of science. No one had any need for my information.

Instead, I was doing the asking as I acquired the skills I eventually would need. I was a stranger in this environment. Even the frost during that fall morning in Massachusetts was a departure from the warmth I had grown accustomed to at my home in Florida. But the experience gave me new insights about other aspects of my life. Just experiencing the feeling associated with that unfamiliar role provided me with a different way of looking at things.

The objective is to discover most emotions are associated with circumstances that often aren't as bad as they initially seem. When I conduct multi-day training programs addressing this subject, I will give participants an assignment to find a partner and do something that's legal and reasonably safe, but that takes them outside their normal comfort zone.

The reason I have them pair up is because there's safety in numbers. Plus, the other person provides the extra motivation that is sometimes needed should one have second thoughts. Examples of the activities people have done include picking up a live snake, wearing outlandish clothes, and bungee jumping.

Some of these tasks may be part of your normal routine. However, for some individuals, doing something for the first time may offer an opportunity to experience emotional discomfort. More importantly, they got over it. That's the key element.

Successfully recovering from adversity is how we learn to be optimistic. "This, too, shall pass" is the lesson learned. And if it's really bad, then from that point on, you can reflect on the experience. Then when confronted with a different type of challenge, say to yourself, "I'm glad I'm not—" (in cold water, bungee jumping, or whatever you did that raised your adrenaline).

Use successive approximation. Take small steps until you feel comfortable leaving your familiar surroundings and making choices with a new set of beliefs. Examine each emotion you experience along with the associated beliefs. By immersing yourself in novel environments, you'll develop the ability to accept and trust yourself, and to gain the confidence to accept change. Armed with those skills, there is no limit to what you will achieve.

Takeaways

- You can be afraid of only those events that haven't happened.
- Fear of failure lessens the motivation to begin tasks.
- Sadness associated with loss is greater than the pleasure associated with gain.
- The greater your knowledge, the less you'll fear.
- Experiencing adversity can build confidence when confronted with setbacks.

4

Because I Can't Help It

Cows, chickens, and rattlesnakes. How can these creatures possibly explain how we form habits and how we can break bad habits? That's my goal in this chapter.

There's another, more challenging barrier to overcome if you tend to delay the start of nearly all projects. It's quite likely your brain has turned the start of any project into the equivalent of Pavlov's bell. You have transformed the routine of putting things off into a habit. Habits involve classical or Pavlovian conditioning in that a sequence of behaviors is set in motion, often with the previous action triggering the next.

Habit Loops

The sequence begins with a trigger. This can be something you see, hear, or smell. It also can be a combination of things. Next, the trigger activates a routine, which will culminate in a reward. The pleasure associated with the arrival of the reward is the third and final part of the habit sequence or habit loop.

Here's an example: Many of us engage in a nocturnal bedroom ritual (closing the curtains, donning pajamas, fluffing the pillow, and perhaps reading a book). It becomes a habit often set in motion by a trigger. For some of us, the trigger might be the conclusion of the nightly news broadcast when the news anchor bids you a good night. It might be something as subtle as the time of day.

In the morning, arrival at the office might be the trigger to visit the breakroom for a cup of coffee, even on days when you might have arisen early and had time for a second cup before leaving home. Putting the coffee cup down becomes associated with walking to your office. Next is checking emails, followed by another coffee break. When you follow that routine every day, then it's probably become your habit loop.

Habits can be highly complex, or as simple a single cue, response, and reward. A simple routine might be grabbing a McFlurry when the McDonald's golden arches come into view. Eventually, it becomes a conditioned habit loop during your daily commute home. The cue is the restaurant, the response is ordering the beverage, and the reward is the sensation elicited by the pleasant taste.

Because this habit loop has become routine, you may not consciously think about why you are pulling up to the drive-through as you lament the fact your clothes are getting tighter. There's nothing wrong with these types of habits. Indeed, they can play an important role in making sure things get done. It's when you engage in a routine for the express purpose of delaying the start of something important that your productivity will be impacted. Now the procrastination label is warranted.

Some people delay all tasks and therefore enable any deadline to trigger a routine of procrastination that eventually runs on autopilot. In much the same way Ivan Pavlov's dogs salivated after associating the sight and smell of meat with a ringing bell, you form unconstructive habits triggered by deadlines. Instead of a bell, your habit is triggered by thoughts associated with completing a task. That includes simple tasks that could be dealt with in short order. Delaying the start of projects, even simple steps, becomes so automatic that, at the end of the day, you realize next to nothing has been accomplished (and so does your boss).

A Habit Is Just a Habit

As far as the brain is concerned, there is no such thing as a good or bad habit. A habit is a habit regardless of the consequences. Whether it's good or bad is a determination we make based on our desires and expectations.

An example of the trigger-behavior-reward loop is something I became a part of after being badly bitten by that alligator at the Black Hills Reptile Gardens in South Dakota. In addition to wrestling alligators, I also milked rattlesnakes. It's how I earned money for college while simultaneously learning about stress! When injured following either an alligator or rattlesnake bite, I would run the Bewitched Village until I was well enough to return to the alligator and snake arenas.

This fictitious village consisted of a gallery of trained animals with cages hidden by a facade resembling an old Western town. When a trained cow received a signal, she would thrust her head from the enclosure and tug a rope attached to a bell. The ringing bell then signaled a half-dozen small chickens to run from their enclosure painted to resemble a house on the prairie to a one-room schoolhouse. Their arrival signaled the school teacher duck to appear.

And so it went with each act cueing the next. A rabbit, goat, and pig each had subsequent roles before the show ended to the delight of the tourists. The trained animal acts comprised the routine, which was triggered by the bell. Each act triggered the next. Once the sequence began, there was no stopping it. It was a metaphor for a complex habit.

Then, one day the initial cue was missing, and the entire show came to a halt.

What started as a normal day ended up a near disaster. I walked onto the stage, turned on the microphone, and began reciting the script to the assembled audience. Next, I sounded the buzzer signaling the cow to ring the bell. But she never appeared. I pressed again. Still no response. Again and again I tried in vain to get the show started. Of course, without the bell, the chickens had no cue to trigger their response, which served as the cue for the next routine and so on. The entire show was dependent on the initial cue.

I had no idea why the cow wasn't responding and couldn't take time to find out. The audience was waiting. Instead, I hurried along the stage, grabbed the rope, and rang the bell myself. But the chickens did not emerge for several moments before sluggishly making their way to the school. That's when I noticed one of the chickens was missing.

When the show finished, I checked backstage and was horrified to discover the reason for what had happened. During the night, raccoons had entered the building and raided the chicken coop. They killed one of the birds, then washed it in the cow's water trough before devouring the remains. Feathers floated on the water and littered the floor. The cow was so traumatized by the brazen nocturnal raid she didn't provide the initial cue. Without the bell the show couldn't start.

This is how you can break the procrastination habit loop. I'm not suggesting you kill a chicken and wash it in the cow's water. But success in changing any habit has to begin by eliminating the cue. The challenge is recognizing success-impeding behaviors for the habit loops they are and then creating a new habit to override it.

The Reward

While the process of forming a habit is straightforward, sustaining it is not. It's one thing to describe the steps on these pages, but translating the instructions into action is not as simple as it might seem. Of course you already know that or you wouldn't be reading this book.

Demands on your time, the sapping of motivation by unexpected incidents, or an abrupt change in the environment (finding a dead chicken on your desk) can serve to disrupt your productivity and completion of tasks. Maybe these disrupters happened to you:

- You overslept the alarm clock.
- You're living out of a suitcase while traveling.
- You've dropped everything to deal with an emergency.
- An illness has sapped your energy.

These are just some of the ways life can throw a monkey wrench into your well-thought-out plans. It's a recipe for stress along with the accompanying emotions, which can interfere with just about everything associated with the good life. Knowing in advance what the potential obstacles are can help you minimize their impact by formulating alternative plans.

Although a habit-triggering cue sets a routine in motion, it's the reward that sustains it. For the animals in the Bewitched Village, it was the food they received upon completion of their routine. At the office, it may be a walk to the employee lounge for coffee and socialization with coworkers that is pleasurable. This routine also serves as a socially acceptable way to delay a potentially monotonous task. It's a pleasurable antidote to boredom. The key to overcoming procrastination is to associate the task you need to complete with something more reward-ing than your delay routine.

There's another problem. Your brain is wired to pri-oritize surviving in the here and now, not in the future. For example, it's well documented that under some forms of severe stress, the chemicals providing energy to deal with a threat will also dampen your immune system. But your brain doesn't care that you might be more vul-nerable to COVID-19 or influenza. That's irrelevant if you're a cadaver. Survive the moment before dwelling on a future that may not materialize.

Furthermore, your brain will guide you to seek rewarding activities. An extensive network of neurons employs the chemicals dopamine and endorphins to pro-duce pleasurable sensations. These can be elicited by eat-ing tasty foods, engaging in sex, exercising, doing drugs such as cocaine, or through a number of other pleasurable experiences. This property of the brain explains why a person might head to the employee lounge for coffee and snacks they don't really want. Their real objective is to delay the monotonous task of reorganizing their boss's massive, disorderly spreadsheet. Pleasure beats boredom every time.

Teenagers are particularly prone to procrastination. Throughout my years in academia, I've lost count of the students who failed an exam because they could barely remain awake after pulling an all-nighter. During the semester they were unable to resist the temptation of par-ties, video games, or hanging out with friends instead of studying. It wasn't difficult because their frontal lobes, a part of the brain that enables a person to associate actions with future rewards and punishments, were still maturing.

To overcome the habit of procrastination, you must connect some entity or occurrence with the project that is more rewarding than the pleasure associated with a coffee break or socializing.

Remember, habits never disappear. They simply get pushed to the inner recesses of the brain after a new one replaces it. However, bad habits often rear their ugly head during times of emotional upheaval. That's because the human brain is wired in a way that favors the familiar. "Better safe than sorry!" is the brain's mantra.

If the stress is great enough, you may revert to habits ingrained in college or during childhood. Some of those routines might have found you turning to alcohol or cigarettes. Back then you might have thought they helped in the short term, but decades later these former habits not only serve no useful purpose, they can be downright unhealthy.

That old habit has been hidden for a lot longer than newer ones, thereby making it more familiar and therefore likely to reappear during times of emotional upheaval. It's one of the reasons people often behave very differently under duress. Next, I'll describe how to replace undesirable habits with habits that will help you achieve goals.

Forming a New Habit

Setting about to begin a new, healthy habit must start with the formation of a cue, like the bell for the cow and the chickens. I'll use as an example losing weight since this is a goal many of us set on New Year's Day, but by the spring have long forgotten. Your approach must be realistic. You're not going to shed all the extra pounds accumulated over the past several years overnight. Indeed, such an approach would be unhealthy and doomed to failure—not to mention disrupting a number of physiological processes.

My recommendation is to start not with the goal of losing weight, but instead to maintain the status quo. Your first objective, then, is to stop gaining weight. The most reliable way to do this is by balancing the intake and expenditure of calories providing you with three options: (1) Reduce the amount and types of foods you consume. (2) Increase your expenditure of calories through exercise. (3) Even better, do both.

Exercise is easy to transform into a habit. You want to simplify the process without a lot of planning or preparation. That means the cue must be something easy to experience. If your schedule allows time for a brisk walk before work, the cue might be your first cup of morning coffee. At first, you'll have to consciously work at this since it's probably not been a part of your routine. But after a while, swallowing the last drop will become associated with setting out on your walk.

Through repetition, the feel of the cup, along with the aroma and taste of coffee, you will acquire properties similar to the bell Pavlov used to automatically stimulate salivation in his dogs. Not a coffee drinker? No worries. Tea, cereal, or whatever else is part of your awakening ritual will work as long as you do the same thing each morning. As soon as you're finished, set out for a brief walk, or if the weather isn't cooperating, an indoor routine such as skipping rope. If you live below a low ceiling, forget the rope. It's the movement that cranks up your heart rate. After a week or two, exercising in the morning will become an automatic response to the cue.

While the ultimate reward will be achieving the desired weight, that's not going to happen for a long time. Perhaps weeks or even months. To make the new routine a habit, it must be followed by an immediate reward. This is where the brain's chemistry can be helpful. Exercise is followed by the release of endorphins. This **end**ogenous **morphine** (your body's drug of choice) induces a feeling of well-being in addition to blunting pain and discomfort. That in itself will be a natural and automatic reward. By the way, extremely fit marathon runners often experience an endorphin high during the run, and you've heard it called the runner's high.

Once you get into shape, endorphins may eventually be released while you're walking, making the routine even more rewarding. Because the reward is such a critical part of forming a new habit loop, you'll need something you directly control so it's guaranteed to be present at the end. Maybe a healthy snack. Chances are the exercise of walking will take the edge off your appetite and result in your eating less than usual.

Furthermore, by carefully selecting the ingredients, you'll be able to obtain the critical nutrients you need, however, packaged with fewer calories. You've now added a guaranteed reward you control to the more variable endorphins. That's a pretty good combination. The challenge will be to carry out this routine regularly.

To meet with success, you must do this every day regardless of what Mother Nature throws your way. That's what accomplished musicians and athletes do. They aren't born with the skills needed to succeed. They have to practice the same routine over and over. Eventually, what they do becomes automatic. The music flows from the fingers of a pianist while she carries on a conversation just as a world-class tennis player doesn't have to think about what he needs to do to return a 100+ mph serve. After years of practice, muscles reflexively contract in response to the rapid input of sensory information. While not the same as the routines underlying habits, these are examples of how the brain can eventually automate a variety of behaviors including habits.

The same principle applies to learning new material. When sitting in the library or your dorm room, you were probably quite adept at juggling classes, mealtimes, and even a part-time job. But then you left all that behind as you worked your way up the ladder to success. Yet when your boss requests you read a lengthy manual to learn a new and complicated software program, you realize you have forgotten how to read to learn, which is very different from reading a novel for pleasure.

The ability to read is not innate. It's a skill, which like all others, must first be acquired and then practiced; if not, your ability to learn will be diminished and perhaps even lost over time. Instead of giving up in frustration, accept the fact your inability to quickly learn the information is most likely from lack of practice, not just a reduction in brain power. I discovered this after taking a decade-long break from academia. Upon returning, it was to teach pre-medical and pre-nursing students anatomy and physiology.

Much had changed during my hiatus in corporate America, including my ability to open a textbook and journals to learn the latest information about the inner workings of the human body. The only benefit I could envision was finding a cure for insomnia! However, during my years working in the lab as a scientist, I couldn't wait to learn the latest breaking news about how the body works. There was excitement as I searched for novel ideas that could be experimentally tested. I'd done it once, so was confident I could do it again.

It required a full semester of relearning to see a return of my ability to whip through a complicated chapter with full comprehension. The most important step was recalling how easy it had been in the past and knowing I could relearn the art of deciphering textbooks. Then, it was a matter of creating rewards.

Upon finishing a section, I'd take a five-minute break. When I'd finish a chapter, I'd balance the time spent reading with a bike ride or walk. I find both these pursuits to be highly pleasurable while simultaneously having time to reflect on what I had read. The key is to break a monotonous task into manageable components with rewarding interludes along the way.

Over the course of several years, the process became a well-ingrained habit and one I found myself looking forward to. The challenge for many people is to ignore the maxim that you can't teach an old dog new tricks. Ding!

So what if you want to break a habit without necessarily substituting a new one? You bite your nails until your fingers are sore, grab a candy bar whenever you walk through the kitchen, or turn on the TV without really thinking about what it is you'll watch?

The first and most important step is to make yourself aware of each time you engage in the habit. You may not even realize you're snacking on your fingertips until nothing remains.

You have several options for breaking habits you may not be aware of. One that is commonly recommended is to keep a rubber band around your wrist and snap it each time you realize you're engaging in the undesirable behavior. At first, you'll do this only once in a while when you happen to experience the awareness. Eventually, the snapping of the band will become associated with the same internal cues that trigger nail-biting.

Another technique is to mark on a piece of paper each time you become aware you're doing what you want to stop. A handheld counter or event tracking app on your smartphone are other ways to heighten your awareness of the habit you are seeking to end.

While the process of forming a habit is straightforward, sustaining it may not be. Demands on your time, the sapping of motivation by unexpected events, or a change in the environment may disrupt a routine before it becomes automatic especially if life threw that monkey wrench at you: you overslept the alarm clock, are temporarily living out of a suitcase while traveling, or are having to deal with an emergency. Knowing such things can happen can help you minimize their impact by planning temporary substitute routines. As long as you are consistent in aligning the cue, routine and reward, you'll make progress strengthening a new habit to override the old and get things done.

Takeaways

- Habits are routines that start with a trigger and are sustained by a reward.
- Habits can be simple or highly complex routines.
- Old habits don't disappear; they are overridden with new ones.
- During stress, older and therefore more familiar habits can emerge.
- Repetition is required to create the cue for a new habit.
- Incorporating a reward into the process of tackling a task you've been delaying is paramount.

5

Because I Don't Believe I Can

All of your life, you've been defining goals and setting objectives to get to where you want to go. But you never seem to arrive. Now, you're going to do something different. You're going to stop, look, and examine those goals you've been setting to determine whether they're connected to your deepest beliefs and values—and if they are not connected, do you need to change your beliefs or your goals to create the necessary match?

If you want to succeed in making positive changes in your life, you must connect your goals with your beliefs. In other words, the way you live your life must be consistent with what is near and dear to you.

What happens when your beliefs are not consistent with the way you are living? Your body finds some way to resist. There will be an undercurrent of regret or sadness perhaps just below conscious awareness. Your immune system may enter a state of withdrawal and thereby leave you susceptible to illness. Perhaps you'll become forgetful or develop high blood pressure. Any conflict between your beliefs and your lifestyle, if allowed to continue, will take a toll on your health.

Sometimes, you need to change your lifestyle—for example, seek a new job or relationship. Other times, it's better to change a belief. If so, start by determining whether your thought is warranted. Where did it come from? Is it really your belief or someone else's? Is it helping you to achieve your goals, or is it hindering your progress?

What Is a Belief?

Merriam-Webster defines belief as "a state or habit of mind in which trust or confidence is placed in some person or thing." Additionally, a belief is defined as "a tenet or body of tenets held by a group."

A belief is an entity in its own right and able to impact many facets of your life from how your cells function in your body to the way you function in relationships. It's important to recognize the origin of your beliefs and to understand how and why you embrace them, especially if a particular belief is detrimental.

You also need to recognize those beliefs you've been ignoring, along with those that have become habits preventing you from living the healthier, happier, enriched life you desire.

With so much polarization in our society these days, it's a worthy exercise to routinely examine our beliefs and their origins.

Let's begin the process by identifying the five main categories of beliefs:

- Core beliefs
- Cultural beliefs
- Hand-me-down beliefs
- Advertised beliefs
- Biological beliefs

Core beliefs are your deepest convictions, sometimes referred to as values. Here's an example of how they can impact life-and-death decisions. It's a comparison of how core beliefs affected the responses of two FBI agents I had an opportunity to meet while lecturing at the FBI National Academy in Quantico, Virginia.

One agent was on a drug stakeout, attempting to apprehend a dealer who was armed with a powerful automatic weapon. The agent, armed with his government-issued pistol, had taken cover behind a wall. Bullets were flying overhead when, suddenly, the shooting stopped. Suspecting the gunman had temporarily run out of ammunition, the agent stood, took aim, and squeezed the trigger. He killed the criminal at a distance of more than 50 yards with a single bullet through the heart.

The other agent was working on a joint task force with a local police jurisdiction. He was sitting at a desk near the door when a deranged gunman came bursting in and began shooting. The agent pulled out his pistol and fired back at a distance of just a few feet. He emptied the clip, but not one of the bullets hit its target. Instead, the agent was shot and almost died from his injuries.

This agent, like all members of his profession, was an excellent marksman.

What was the difference?

The agent involved in the drug bust had played competitive sports throughout his schooling. Under stress, his body automatically reverted to a familiar way of responding, based on a core belief that it was important to always win. He had an attitude that said, "I'm not going to let that guy beat me. I'm going to win this contest," and that's how he approached any challenging situation. While under fire he experienced the same familiar feeling experienced on the sports field. He reflexively went into a competitive stance under pressure.

The other agent had never participated in competitive sports. He lacked that competitive edge. He was also a religious man who may have felt that it was wrong to take another person's life. Although he would have been in full compliance with the Office of the Attorney General's deadly force policy had he killed the criminal, to do so would have been in violation of his personal deadly force policy. This he acknowledged during a post-incident inquiry.

I'm not suggesting that there is anything wrong with the second agent's belief, or that a competitive approach to problems is always better. Problems arise when there is a mismatch between your belief-driven behavior and the environment in which you find yourself. You may never be in a shootout with a drug dealer, but you need to know what your core beliefs are and avoid putting yourself in a position where your work or lifestyle may conflict with those beliefs. And you need to understand how deeply connected those beliefs are to your emotional brain, which, in turn, can impact your susceptibility to pain and illness.

Is your marriage heading toward divorce court? Are you up to your neck in debt? Do you toss and turn at night unable to sleep? If your answer is yes, it's little wonder you are unable to achieve goals. This inner turmoil is keeping you in withdrawal mode, which is keeping you from completing even small tasks. Moving forward may require jump-starting your system by examining the core beliefs shaping your decisions.

Cultural beliefs are those beliefs woven into the culture you were raised in. They may also be core beliefs and capable of working for or against you. Let me give you an example.

Without warning, a healthy, twenty-eight-year-old Philippine American woman was impaired with aching joints. Her face became inflamed and discolored, especially when she went into the sunlight. Her immune system was engaged in a form of friendly fire. Instead of attacking viruses and bacteria, it was targeting her own otherwise healthy cells. Diagnosed with an autoimmune disease called systemic lupus erythematosus, she was given drugs to suppress her runaway immune system. But the medication didn't work, in part because she didn't believe in either the treatment or in the powers of the Western-trained physicians.

Her doctor recommended a more aggressive course of treatment using higher doses and more frequent administration of the drug. She rejected that advice and returned to her native Philippines. Upon arrival, she sought the counsel of the witch doctor who had treated her as a child. Instead of giving her more drugs, he removed a curse that had been placed on her by a former suitor.

When she returned to the US, the same physician who had made the original diagnosis concluded her lupus was in full remission.

Two aspects are remarkable about this case report. First, it was not published in a grocery-store tabloid. Instead, it was reported in the highly regarded *Journal of the American Medical Association*. Second, neither the author of the case report, Dr. Richard Kirkpatrick, nor the editorial staff of the journal questioned whether the witch doctor succeeded after the practitioner of Western medicine appeared to have failed. Rather, the question posed at the end of the article was "By what mechanism had the witch doctor succeeded?"

But did the ethnic healer really succeed in ridding her of her lupus? The patient most likely had a mild form of the disease, which had remained in remission for most of her life. It was only when her belief in the power of a curse disrupted her biochemistry that the symptoms of lupus were able to emerge. The witch doctor did not cure the woman of lupus; he cured her of her anxiety, which only he could do in her culture.

So instead of being an example of the power of one type of healing tradition over another, this case serves as a wonderful example of the power belief-driven emotions can have in shifting the delicate balance between good health and disease.

You acquire cultural beliefs from a number of sources including family, friends, religious institutions, and with organizations with which you identify. Cultural beliefs can be very strong and can run deeply. Furthermore, the earlier you're exposed to such a belief, the more strongly it will be ingrained, and the more difficult it will be to get rid of. It may shape your thought processes and behaviors in a manner similar to the wire restraints that shape the branches of a bonsai tree.

Hand-me-down beliefs may come from any source, but most often they come to us from our parents or grandparents during our early childhood. This is a time during the life cycle when we are most impressionable.

Such beliefs can affect our career choices. Maybe you wanted to be a writer or an artist, but you always heard, "You can't make a living painting or writing." Relationships can be impacted, "If you want it done right, do it yourself." And even change, "You can't teach an old dog new tricks." Just a chance statement at the dinner table when you were ten years old might have instilled a belief capable of guiding all future decisions, along with the motivation to pursue or discount career-shaping choices.

My entire life has been changed by a hand-me-down belief, which turned out to be wrong. At the impressionable age of seven, I had arrived home from school devastated over having failed a math exam. The school I attended in England was a carryover from the Dickens era, where students were caned across the hand with a bamboo stick for doing poorly on exams or not completing homework assignments. It was a very strict school. There had already been the physical punishment, followed by the belief I was a failure. I was an emotional wreck.

My mother, a wonderful lady whom I loved dearly, tried to console me by saying, "Don't worry about it. No one in our family has ever done well in math." And I thought, "YES! It's not my fault. I just chose the wrong parents. It's those darned ancestors who gave me a defective genetic blueprint."

From that moment, I stopped applying myself in math. I expended just enough effort to keep from getting caned, and that was about it. When I barely passed the course, I was happy as a clam. Instead, I focused on those classes I did enjoy and that I did well in. The belief I was not and would never be good at math shaped my selection of courses for more than a decade.

It wasn't until I attended graduate school where I had to take statistics followed by advanced statistics that I realized I had been making choices in response to an erroneous belief. With the help of an excellent instructor, I realized that not only is math not all that difficult, but it's important to understand. In my case, it was going to be a valuable tool enabling me to analyze research data I would be collecting in my chosen profession as a psychoneuroimmunologist.

I've often wondered how my life might have been notably different had it not been for my mother's well-intended and consoling words. I might have become a CPA or an accountant. I might be working for the IRS, auditing your tax return and causing you stress, instead of writing books about how to deal with the subsequent emotions.

To this day, I tend to delay starting tasks involving numbers. Despite knowing that filling out tax returns is not difficult, I often file for an extension because I know I'll miss the deadline. Perhaps it's because of the boredom I experience while filling out forms after reviewing seemingly endless receipts. However, I can't help wonder whether it's in part because I'm being influenced by remnants of a childhood belief. As I said earlier, it's during times of stress that the old and more familiar beliefs and habits resurface.

Advertised beliefs. Let's now examine how advertisements we are bombarded with influence our choices. Consider the word *stress*. It's used as a noun ("I have stress."), a verb ("I am stressed."), and an adjective ("I have stress-induced pain."). And no matter how you use it, it usually has a negative connotation. I'm sure you've heard that stress is bad for you. It's one of the most promoted myths in our culture, and it sells more books, magazines, and audio programs than even sex these days.

In actuality, stress is good for you. It's a stimulus for physical, emotional, and spiritual growth. Problems arise when we fail to balance stress with recovery. Stress is the stimulus for the growth, which takes place during recovery.

Another widely advertised belief pertains to the immune system. Lots of advertised beliefs within the health industry promote the benefits of augmenting your immune system. Echinacea, golden seal, and green tea are just a few of the many over-the-counter drugs people consume in an effort to boost their immune systems. Why do they do this? Because it is an advertised belief that boosting the immune system is the magical solution for all health problems.

It's not.

Too much of the wrong kind of immunity characterizes people with multiple sclerosis or rheumatoid arthritis. Too much of another form of immunity is the cause of severe allergies. Nonetheless, this widely advertised belief has helped the health food and supplement industry become a multi-billion-dollar-a-year business.

While the immune system is not usually associated with procrastination, the pain and discomfort associated with the consequences of immune system imbalance are. So is the lack of energy, which is a common symptom associated with some of the chemicals released during an immune response. Instead of addressing the question, I know what to do, so why won't I do it? many physiologic abnormalities align more with the related question: I know what to do, so why *can't* I do it?

Biological beliefs. Another impediment to achieving goals is one I call a biological belief, although it's related more to classical conditioning than it is to the beliefs discussed thus far. These subconscious beliefs are able to provoke responses, but which dwell below the conscious radar.

You may not remember the salad you had for lunch prior to the serious car crash you were in. Or the country music song playing on the radio when the phone rang and you learned of the unexpected death of a loved one. But now, every time your body is exposed to those cues, you experience the same fear or sadness that occurred at the time of the event. Of course, sometimes the opposite can occur.

A birthday, pizza restaurant, or photo may elicit memories of over-the-top ecstasy for someone you deeply love and care about. It's a conditioned response, which is a form of learning. You also can think of this as a biological belief. Without any conscious awareness, your body believes the same circumstances exist, and it responds accordingly. In a subtle way, feelings triggered by such beliefs could be keeping you from doing the things you should be doing by triggering withdrawal-inducing emotions such as sadness or fear.

I am sometimes asked to testify as an expert witness in legal cases involving posttraumatic stress disorder. I remember one case, in particular, because it was so disheartening. A beautiful young woman had been brutally assaulted. It happened in a car, and, thereafter, that brand of automobile, the song playing on the radio, and even that fragrance she had been wearing triggered a response so powerful that it set off the same autoimmune system illness experienced by the Philippine American woman who was plagued by a different type of curse.

Beliefs That Hold You Back

"I know what to do, so why don't I do it?" Probably because you don't believe you can. Here are some beliefs (excuses) people use to explain why they don't engage in healthy pursuits such as exercise or healthy eating, but they can also apply to any belief that holds you back. Many were passed on to me by clinical caseworkers, while others I've heard when presenting seminars to healthcare professionals.

- I am too busy.
- I don't have the time to shop for the right foods.
- I work too many hours to be able to exercise.
- I have children at home to take care of.
- I can't keep track.
- I have too many family problems.
- Healthy eating is expensive.
- I don't need to exercise because I'm on my feet all day at work.
- I have low metabolism so I can't lose weight.
- I am under too much stress at work.
- My family cooks all the foods I like, and I can't refuse.
- I don't know what healthy choices are.
- I can't stick to a strict diet.
- I live in a dangerous neighborhood so can't exercise.
- I lost the list of foods I need to stay away from.
- I don't like any of the foods that are good for me.
- With the holidays, it is impossible to stick to my routine.

- I'm not the one who buys the groceries.
- I have too many other health problems.
- I'm too old.
- I have tried every kind of exercise and diet. Nothing works.
- I just take extra insulin if I eat too much.
- My doctor never told me to lose weight.
- My scales are broken.
- My exercise bike is broken.
- I am hungry all the time.
- I am bored so I eat all day long.
- It's too painful to exercise.
- It's inconvenient.
- I don't have time.
- It's boring.
- It's hard to keep up.
- I'm too out of shape.

These listed reasons/excuses can be organized into six distinct categories:

- Lack of time (I'm too busy.)
- Lack of money (Eating healthy is too expensive.)
- Lack of knowledge (I don't know what healthy choices are.)
- Lack of ability (I have too much pain to exercise.)
- Lack of motivation (I know what to do. I just don't do it.)
- Lack of optimism (It is too late, and I'm too old to change.)

Upon further inspection, these six distinct types of excuses correspond to the three major constituents of a person: mind, body, and spirit.

Mind: Insufficient knowledge is a function of the mind. So is perceived lack of time, of which you have plenty. The problem is how you prioritize what you do with what's available.

Body: Having a multitude of health problems can represent a formidable obstacle. While it doesn't directly cause disease, stress can create an environment within the body making it easier for the causes of disease to rear their ugly heads.

Spirit: Lacking the will to change can be an insurmountable obstacle if not dealt with. So is a feeling of pessimism. Chances are, it's a belief that's holding you back.

Some of these explanations are legitimate. It's difficult to engage in healthy pursuits when you're struggling financially to make it one day at a time. However, others may be used to justify procrastination.

Changing Unhealthy Beliefs

Whenever you encounter a belief (whether it's a core belief, a cultural belief, a hand-me-down belief, or an advertised belief), answer these questions. I'm going to ask them in the context of how they affect your relationship with yourself, your family, your business associates, your neighbors, as well as the community. And dig deep for the answers. Plan to spend considerable time reflecting on each and don't assume that whatever comes to mind first is the only answer.

- Are these your beliefs or those of someone else?
- Are your beliefs based on experience?
- Can you think of times in your life when your belief was challenged by reality?
- Have your beliefs ever kept you from achieving a goal?
- Are certain themes reflected in your beliefs?
- Are you willing to change one or more of your beliefs if they are obstacles to your goals?
- Are your beliefs serving a useful purpose?

You don't have to wait. Begin the process right now by identifying a belief you would like to change. Pick one that is holding you back. Here's an example: Better safe than sorry. People are afraid of failure so they play it safe in both their personal and professional lives. You must overcome this belief if you are to be successful.

Any change requires moving away from familiar territory, which carries with it the risk of failure. No wonder people stay where they are. Even though their business venture could have the potential of doubling its profits, they either delay making an advantageous choice until the opportunity is lost, or they decide to remain in the same old rut job. We hold onto a belief because we have become set in our ways. We may want to do things differently, but we fear change. We are afraid of failing. So instead of taking steps to improve our lot, we keep things status quo. We even create new beliefs to justify inaction.

I have a friend who services clients for a large company. His job requires that he log up to 50,000 miles a year driving throughout the Eastern US. Every hour he is on the road, he is away from his family and those things in life that bring him pleasure. Then he was offered a promotion. Not only did it come with a higher salary, but a short commute from his home to company headquarters. "No way," he told me. "I'm not going to become part of that rat race. Too much back biting at headquarters. I'd rather be on my own, even if it means a lower salary and eating in truck stops."

Where does this belief come from? Perhaps from his early childhood. Many men are taught that they must be decisive and always make the right decision. Role models may have been present in the family or depicted on television by our childhood heroes. Or perhaps through the pages of books read to us by parents. Subtle messages conveying what a hero can and should be were present throughout our early upbringing.

What happens, though, when the child encounters failure and realizes that success is not guaranteed? Fear of failure causes the person to avoid situations requiring them to accept more responsibility. The person might seek employment in a subservient position so someone else can shoulder the responsibility for failure. Not only will this belief impact their professional life, but they may also select a partner who plays a dominant role in a personal relationship.

While in some cases it might be necessary to consult with a therapist to help with the process, by asking the right questions, you can often identify for yourself what is triggering a particular behavioral path. Just understanding the cause of your lack of action may be all that's needed to take the first step toward change.

At Saddlebrook Resort in Florida, I teach corporate clients to accept the inevitable risks that always accompany success. These lessons are best taught in an environment where challenges can be created through realistic scenarios. Ours is a five-acre facility, which includes a climbing wall, zip line, and other initiatives built high in the trees. The participants may be instructed to solve complex tasks on the ground, or to get their team across a rope bridge they have to build across an expanse of water. Some activities may also involve actors playing the role of difficult clients or disgruntled employees. The participants learn to trust one another and to communicate under pressure.

Our own research, as well as that of others, has revealed improved self and group efficacy immediately upon completion of the day's training. Furthermore, there is an increase in trust and a decrease in stress. Corporations improve their bottom line, and, by having healthier and more productive team members, their shareholders welcome this type of investment. Because of demand, we now are signing up families and engaged couples who use the program to enrich their relationships. Why? Because it works, it's fun, and can be accomplished in just half a day.

You can take steps to overcome obstructive beliefs without going through experiential training or building a rope bridge. Begin by asking the belief-related questions listed earlier in this chapter and repeated here:

- Are these your beliefs or those of someone else?
- Are your beliefs based on experience?
- Can you think of times in your life when your belief was challenged by reality?
- Have your beliefs ever kept you from achieving a goal?
- Are certain themes reflected in your beliefs?
- Are you willing to change one or more of your beliefs if they are obstacles to your goals?
- Are your beliefs serving a useful purpose?

You are the only one who can answer these questions. Write down your answers and then read them out loud. Sometimes, when you receive information via multiple sensory modalities, it's easier to process and to understand. Contemplate all the beliefs impacting your life, and then when pondering if a given belief is justified, reflect upon previous occasions when that belief influenced your decisions. What was the outcome? Even if you weren't successful, was the outcome really all that bad? Bad enough to prompt you never again to attempt to move forward?

And while you are at it, which decisions do you most regret? Those you made or those you didn't? Then list all of the ways your life may change if you accept the challenge of changing your belief and succeed? Bear in mind, there is no single correct answer to any of the listed questions.

The primary purpose of this exercise is to have a framework within which to examine your beliefs. Having done so, you will be better prepared to choose between the two key options you should always start with: you can change your belief, or you can change the environment.

Sometimes changing the environment may be the best choice. If you are being asked in the workplace to do something dishonest or otherwise counter to your core beliefs, it clearly is a good idea to seek another job. Or perhaps your marriage has become so destructive that divorce is the only sensible option. That can be an extremely difficult decision because you may have a guilt-driven compulsion to keep returning to try and make it work. Such futile efforts may be driven by a belief that giving up is always bad or from an unwillingness to initiate change because, despite the turmoil, you are at least familiar with the status quo.

I was faced with a similar dilemma at the university where I was once employed. The difference was my desire to change another person's belief. After several years of success, my mind-body research program was regarded by my chairman as a bad fit for his department. I didn't understand his rationale. The program was well funded by federal grants, my students were winning national recognition, prestigious medical schools were implementing similar programs, and I had recently been promoted to the rank of professor. My chairman's belief made no sense to me, just as my persistence to remain probably made no sense to him.

I hung in there until the bitter end, trying in vain to change another person's belief to be consistent with my own. I felt leaving would constitute failure on my part—a form of giving up. "There must be something I can do to change his mind," I kept thinking.

It took a long time, but eventually I accepted the fact that you cannot control another person's beliefs or actions. You can only control your own. So I finally changed the environment and left. Afterward, my only regret was not having made the change when the mismatch between our two beliefs and the environment first surfaced. (Redemption came when that chairman was subsequently fired for sexual misconduct, and I was recruited to return to the same university.)

Is my belief justified? You have to ask this question in every situation. The belief that a reasonable and swift punishment is beneficial may be justified when teaching a child the difference between right and wrong. But that same belief may be totally inappropriate in the office where it may be advantageous to encourage others to take the risks required to achieve a new level of success. In the next chapter, I'll discuss the impact your beliefs exert when defining and achieving your lifelong goals.

Takeaways

- Your beliefs must be aligned with your values.
- Regularly scrutinize your beliefs to determine their validity.
- The excuses we create to avoid achieving goals are grounded in beliefs.
- Beliefs can arise from a variety of sources. What matters is that they contribute to your happiness and success.
- Emotions can be triggered by both conscious and subconscious beliefs.
- Beliefs and past experiences shape the mental images that give rise to the choices you make.

6

Because I Don't Know
What I Want

When you introduce yourself to someone and have to give a one or two sentence description of who you are, do you answer like this?

"Hi. I'm Nick Hall, Director of Important Stuff at the XYZ Corporation."

Is your identity attached to your work? If so, you might have too much of your self-esteem—of who you are as a person—tied to the workplace. If one day you awaken and are no longer Director of Important Stuff at the XYZ Corporation, who would you be? If you lost your job tomorrow, how would you define yourself? You could no longer say, "I'm Director of Important Stuff." You could no longer say, "I work at the XYZ Corporation."

Consider these options: Are you a daughter, a brother, a mother, a son? Are you a sailor, a gardener, a banker, a woodworker, an artist? Your personal identity will, in turn, shape your values and beliefs, which will impact your progress toward achieving a goal.

If your beliefs are enabling you to make progress toward achieving your goals, then it's likely the emotions you experience are largely positive and fulfilling. But if your beliefs are keeping you from achieving your goals, you're probably harboring negative emotions. And if you don't know what your beliefs or goals are, then you probably bounce from one emotional state to another without knowing why.

Why is it that some people live life so passionately and so fully? They work at jobs they love. They enjoy their family. They have mastered the art of pleasure. They are rich in every aspect of their life because they are living it to their fullest potential. It's most likely their choices and lifestyle reflect their core beliefs and values.

Discovering What You Value

As I travel the country presenting workshops on mind/ body issues, I find that most people don't really believe they can be whatever they want to be, or live their dream. Their beliefs won't allow them to accept this. I find, too, that many people don't really value what they are currently doing, nor the things they have. And it's not for lack of trying.

Do you know people who go to seminar after seminar? Who read self-help books and obediently complete the assignments they learn when listening to audio programs or podcasts, yet they still can't seem to put it all together to make the necessary changes? Even if they get a better job, they are still not happy. Oh, they might be happy for a while, but the same problems seem to resurface at work and at home. When these problems involve finances, which they often do, the person becomes angry, afraid, fearful, or ashamed.

Their actions, the way they live, the jobs they accept are not congruent with their core beliefs. And because their beliefs are in conflict with their lifestyle, it affects their emotional state in ways that are highly detrimental to their physical and mental health. It affects how they feel about themselves, the way they eat, whether or not they exercise, what they do for a living, the quality of their family life, and how they plan for the future. Remember, emotions arising from events in your personal life can spill over and have a direct impact on your professional goals and well-being. The opposite is also true: emotions triggered at the office can bear upon your family life.

How do you know who you are and what you really believe is important? Here's a fun way to find out what's near and dear to you. Imagine you have just discovered you selected the winning numbers in a lottery and have received a check for $10 million. But there's a catch. You have five minutes to decide what to do with it—every last penny. And what you don't spend, you don't get. Start writing, and remember, you have only five minutes.

What immediately comes to mind? New house, new car, new clothes? You might turn to advertised beliefs (discussed in the previous chapter) associated with what success should look like. Perhaps you'll be guided by what someone else has told you being rich should look like. Be careful. You may be spending your money and redesigning your life based on somebody else's values. What about buying things for someone else? A mansion for your parents, a Mercedes for your best friend, a sport fishing boat for your brother-in-law, and an all-expenses-paid dream vacation for a couple of friends?

What's up with the big spender? Just being a nice person? Look closer. It could very well be a hand-me-down belief. Maybe you think you don't deserve the money, and you need to give it away. Or you've heard that rich people aren't nice; they're miserly. So you give the windfall away instead of becoming like that. Or maybe, as a child, you never had enough money, so you're going to spend everything you have to show off your good fortune.

Look at your lottery list. Is there a charitable organization on your list or did you immediately invest it to make more money? What does this say about your values? Think carefully. Do you really need the purchases, or are you spending or not spending money in a way that is expected of you? What if you are unable to develop a list for all of this money? You have no idea what to do with it?

Don't mistake the objective of this exercise. The intent is not to instill a particular belief. It's to get you thinking about what you value. There is no right or wrong belief. It's only when a belief is not justified or impedes progress toward a worthwhile goal that it needs to be changed.

Take a break from reading and complete the following statements in a manner consistent with your beliefs and values.

1. Life is_____. A cynic might answer a terminal disease. A more positive response might be a precious gift.

2. The world would be a better place to live if_____. There are no illnesses? How about if there is more goodwill?

3. And here's one more example, which gets to the core of this exercise. I am_____.

Are you still uncertain about what it is you value? Do you value money, power, labor, authority, or competence? Or, perhaps, family, your career, or material possessions? It matters less what you value. What's important is that you *know* what it is you value.

Create Your Blueprint

Here's another way to find out what you value. Reflect for a moment upon that one person in your life—a grandparent, parent, close friend, or a mentor—who always seems to make the right decision, no matter how much pressure they're under. Someone whose behavior you have tried to emulate when you've found yourself facing difficult circumstances.

How would you describe this person? What words come to mind that characterize this person you look up to? Chances are this person reflects your own beliefs and values. Often, when I ask that question of audiences, their answers include the words *balanced, controlled, confident, compassionate, caring, flexible, energized, calm,* and *peaceful.*

Do those sound like the words on your list? If these are the common characteristics of people you admire, then they are probably the characteristics that you most value and desire to have yourself. You can become that person if you aren't already. The important first step is to experience the realization of who you want to be. Let's look closely at that list again.

Balanced. These are people who don't just talk the talk; they walk the walk. They have a good balance of time spent at work and with family. They eat healthfully and exercise. They relax and play. They are involved in their communities. They have plenty of social interactions, yet they take the time to reflect and allow time for themselves. They live a balanced life. Most importantly, they conduct their lives in a manner that is consistent with their beliefs and value system. They don't deviate. Their value system is like an old friend, a constant that keeps them centered, even during the most severe stress.

Controlled. These people are in control. But, by control, I do not mean having the desire to manipulate or control other people. Instead, they are in control of their own emotions and don't allow anger, fear, or sadness to interfere with their pursuit of goals. They are driven by values-aligned beliefs that serve as a cornerstone for their lives.

Confident. These people are able to do things with seemingly little effort. As a consequence they exude confidence. In addition, they are able to instill confidence in others, which is why people often gravitate to them.

Compassionate and caring. They believe in the inherent good in all people. They do not prejudge others.

Flexible and energized. They are active physically as well as mentally. They are open-minded people who gather as much information as they can so their perception of the world is realistic.

Calm and peaceful. They have core beliefs that match their system of living. Their way of life reflects what they believe. They are in their optimal emotional state—that condition when the emotion they feel and express will help propel them toward a worthwhile goal. They are healthy as they work and live to their fullest potential. They also have maximum functional capacity right up until the end of their life.

What prevents you from accessing this optimal emotional state?

First, think of the times you have been able to access this state when everything seemed to flow effortlessly. You thought clearly, performed optimally, and accomplished more. You were relaxed and felt good about yourself and what you were doing. Maybe it happened once on the golf course—one of those days where you just couldn't miss. Perhaps it was the time you organized a large family reunion and pulled it off flawlessly, or wrote a paper during which the words flowed from your fingertips. Remember those times when you weren't anxious or frustrated. You were balanced, controlled, confident, compassionate, caring, flexible, energized, calm, and peaceful.

What stops you from accessing this state more often? What prevents you from acquiring those qualities you most admire in your favorite person? An erroneous belief?

Here are some of the most common excuses I've heard, which, invariably, are not justified and impede progress toward a goal.

- I'm awkward in crowds.
- I never do well on tests.
- There's nothing I can do about it.
- It runs in my family.
- Failure is bad; I must always succeed.
- Stress is bad, and it should be avoided.
- I'm too old to change.
- I'm no good at relationships.
- Nice guys finish last.

Some beliefs may be difficult to change, especially if cultural. Examine your workplace culture. Is there pressure to work a tremendous amount of overtime to get ahead? Do you believe that if you tell colleagues you are taking off early to see your daughter in a play or to celebrate your wedding anniversary, they won't take you seriously?

I know workplaces where it's considered a badge of courage not to take a vacation. People are proud of having stored 100 or more unused vacation days. Some people proudly display million-mile tags on their airline baggage. To me, it says the time they spend on their work is out of proportion with time spent with family, with community, and with self. And I know they are not nearly as productive as they think they are. They are driven by some of the common beliefs ingrained in their work culture, instead of their own value system.

For just a moment, project your mind in space and time to the future. I know this is a bit morbid, but when you are lying on your deathbed, in your hour of final reflection, do you think that you're going to wish you'd spent more time at the office, or more time with your friends and family?

Let's now consider advertised beliefs and the concept of balance. Picture this. There's a man at Disney World with his family turning on his cell phone to check in with work. Cut to a new scene: a woman having lunch with her mother at a lovely restaurant, but she has her notebook computer on the table, checking social media. Almost all advertisements surrounding technology want you to believe that you can have more downtime because you can be connected with work while you relax. This is a contradiction.

You need to unplug, unwind, and just relax when you relax. Enjoy nothing else but the art in the museum when you are there. And don't miss out on the great conversation over lunch with your mom. Be where you are. That's an important part of living a centered life. When your life is in balance, your access to the optimal emotional state is easy and effortless.

Where Are You Going?

Now that you've reflected on your beliefs and value system, what do you want to do with them? What do you want out of life? Many people live their entire life without ever asking this question, and, as a consequence, they fail to accomplish all that they might have.

A childhood prayer concludes, "If I should die before I wake, I pray the Lord my soul to take." A sad thought. Just as sad would be the substitution of these words: "If I should die before I live." Too many people drift aimlessly throughout the decades without a clear understanding of what they truly want. They eventually die at a ripe old age, but without having truly lived. More than likely, they never had any meaningful goals.

Don't let this happen to you. Identify your personal goals now. Complete these statements, and do so on a regular basis, so you don't forget.

- In my lifetime, I want to _____
- Prior to retirement, I want to _____
- Before my children leave home to pursue their own goals, I want to _____
- By _____, I want to _____

Now ask yourself these questions:

- Are these goals attainable?
- Are they my goals or those of someone else?

- Are they stated concisely and as a positive objective?
- Am I willing to begin now? If not, under what circumstances will I begin?
- Am I willing to make changes in my life to achieve my goals?
- Are my goals consistent with my values and beliefs?
- Do any of my goals conflict with each other?
- What am I willing to give up to achieve my goals?

Establishing unrealistic goals is a sure way to failure. And don't forget, it's your life. Do what feels right for you, not what you think is expected of you by associates or by family members.

You also must make a commitment to achieve your goals. Many people get involved in various projects that they believe will guide them to the good life, but they fail to get there because they don't make a commitment. True commitment means making sacrifices and delaying gratification. Establishing unrealistic goals is an effort in futility. And identifying goals that are inconsistent with your values and beliefs will produce a constant source of conflict.

Ten Beliefs That Can Block Your Progress

Some beliefs based on biases or faulty perceptions interfere with growth and personal happiness, regardless of the environment. Often these beliefs are learned during childhood and are reinforced throughout life. We know intellectually that these perspectives are faulty, but we have difficulty changing due to the strong emotions associated with the underlying belief. Often these beliefs are so ingrained that we use them without thinking, despite the fact they can lead to feelings of sadness, hopelessness, fear, or anxiety.

Following are ten common beliefs many people grapple with. As you review them, ask yourself which of these beliefs preside over your life.

1. **I must be loved, validated, and approved by everyone.** This belief keeps you from being yourself out of fear you will meet with disapproval or rejection. Individuals who subscribe to this belief often cheat themselves out of being who they are, focusing instead on evaluating situations and other people for how to respond. As a result, difficulties in both professional and personal relationships are common because a healthy relationship requires two separate individuals who respect their own and each other's identity.

2. **I am responsible for other people.** By taking responsibility for others, you may inadvertently take away their motivation to accept responsibility for themselves. In addition, you put yourself in a no-win situation. Controlling other people is rarely, if ever, possible. When you do this, you lose touch with yourself.

3. **My success and happiness depend on other people and events I have no control over.** Feeling helpless is a formula for seldom achieving your full potential. So is having a sense of being too much in control and accepting responsibility for everything that happens to you. Basically, when things are going well and you're making progress toward your goal, you want to have a strong sense of being involved and of being a part of the process. "I worked hard to achieve outstanding results and completed everything asked of me on time. I earned my promotion and raise." A person who would make such a statement has a strong sense of being in control; something that psychologists refer to as an internal locus of control.

The opposite attitude is reflected in this statement: "It doesn't matter what or how well I do, I'll never get ahead. It's the big shots in the top floor offices who make all the decisions based on politics and the bottom line. What I do never makes any difference."

When things do go well, this person is likely to declare his raise had nothing to do with his work, it was because the company needed a tax deduction. This person has an external locus of control. However, like many things in life, the healthy person will achieve a happy medium. "I did all I could to achieve the objective, but, ultimately, insurmountable obstacles arose due to events outside my control."

4. **I must be the best at everything I do—I can't make mistakes.** Perfectionism is a battle that many people

fight every day. It's important to accept that every-body has areas of strength and weakness. To be human is to be imperfect. While everybody likes to excel, no one can possibly excel at everything. Most successful people have succeeded only after many failures or mistakes.

Life is a learning experience. Some people can-not acknowledge an imperfection because they never received the love and support to feel comfortable with their shortcomings. Deep down, they feel worthless and end up making unreasonable demands on them-selves and sometimes on others. In that unrealistic, overdemanding world, they are able to justify their belief that there's no point in doing what they know they should. Then, in order to feel good about them-selves, they'll project their faults onto other individ-uals or groups and blame them for whatever goes wrong. In short, when they criticize others, they are really revealing their own shortcomings.

If you believe each day should be perfect and that everything you do is flawless, you are going to have very low self-esteem as you constantly fail to achieve this unrealistic standard. By the way, per-fectionism is okay in some environments. It's good that engineers at NASA are perfectionists, and you certainly want your surgeon to adhere to the high-est standards possible. Problems arise when the perfection required in some environments is unre-alistically applied to all.

5. **I can avoid dealing with problems or pain in life.** While you can postpone addressing difficulties and pain in life, you cannot avoid tough times indefinitely. Accepting them and dealing with problems and emotions directly allows you to put them behind you. Avoiding emotions is rarely effective for the long term. It's not possible to fully enjoy positive feelings when you have denied negative feelings. It is the failure to acknowledge an emotion that will wreak havoc on your life.

   I'm not suggesting that you walk into your boss's office and engage in a form of emotional exhibitionism. Carefully choose the right time and place. Remember, the emotion is signaling an unmet need that needs to be addressed. Denying the emotion is ignoring the problem. You have a choice. You can deal with it consciously on your terms, or you can wait for it to surprise you when your body can't take it anymore. (In a previous chapter, I described how stress has the potential to derail your immune system and weaken your heart.)

6. **Inconveniences in life are catastrophes.** It's important to keep the daily hassles and inconveniences in life in proper perspective. What is the worst-case scenario? Is it really as bad as you fear? Life is full of unexpected challenges. Your choice is to either accept this fact or repeatedly set yourself up for disappointment by expecting life to be hassle-free. Paradoxically,

when you accept this fact, the hassles become easier to tolerate.

7. **I must be in control at all times.** There are many things in life beyond our control. However, we are consistently in control of our attitude. If we believe in the illusion of control, we will repeatedly face the impossible task of trying to govern what is beyond our ability. While it is beneficial to maintain control over situations that we can influence, the belief that we have power over all events is an illusion that is responsible for much unhappiness.

It's good to have control over some things. Problems arise when control becomes the end instead of the means, when we refuse to relinquish it even when circumstances call for delegation or simply letting go. Reinhold Niebuhr said it best: "God, grant me the serenity to accept the things I cannot change, courage to change the things I can, and wisdom to know the difference."

8. **If people knew the real me, they would not like me.** This belief can cause you to pretend to be someone you are not, ultimately distancing yourself from other people including those who might truly appreciate and enjoy the person you really are. The bad news is that you probably do have some traits or features others might find undesirable. The good news is that everyone has traits that others might find objectionable.

Furthermore, when you recognize your own limitations, it becomes easier to accept those of others. You'll be more realistic and not expect them to be better than they really are. Furthermore, you'll have less tendency to exaggerate the negative.

9. **It is wrong to enjoy myself too much.** While life is sometimes painful and difficult, it is healthy to enjoy life and to seek fulfillment and joy when the opportunity arises. Once you accept this, you become closer to and appreciate more the people around you.

10. **I can't change because I've always been the way I am.** If you truly believe this, it is unlikely you will change because you have sealed yourself off. Choices are made each and every moment in life. While changing can be difficult, you effect change by making choices. What characterizes truly healthy people is having the capacity to deal with change. Some people thrive on it as they view events not as obstacles but as challenges. Many people can't seem to maintain openness and flexibility, and they end up distraught when things don't turn out as they expected. For these people, even minor changes can make them feel overwhelmed.

Any of these ten beliefs can interfere with your professional development and personal enrichment. They will keep you from achieving goals by giving rise to unhealthy emotions and inappropriate responses. Not only that, but eventually your beliefs may become a self-fulfilling prophecy. You put off starting important projects so often, procrastination becomes your automatic response to even simple tasks.

There are no quick remedies for dealing with many of the beliefs we embrace because, as described earlier, there are no good and bad beliefs. Problems arise when a belief is not aligned with your values and personal goals. As was true with the beliefs that impede achieving short-term and work-related goals, the solution lies within you. No one else can determine if a belief is justified, serving a useful purpose, or feels right.

Takeaways

- Your values are the core of who you are.
- Verify that your values are aligned with your beliefs.
- Create a strategic plan for reaching your lifelong personal goals.
- Be mindful of counterproductive beliefs.
- Be willing to make changes while in pursuit of your goals.
- Make certain your personal goals are yours and not being sought to please others.

7

Because I Can't Do Anything Right

The previous chapters have dealt with the ability of emotions and beliefs to influence if and when you set about to achieve a goal. So where do those beliefs and emotions originate? Instead of tackling these entities after they appear, is there a way to influence them before they come to pass? There is.

The headwaters of all our responses, whether behavioral or emotional, lie within the parts of the brain that give rise to our perception of events.

It begins with the arrival in the brain of sensory information and its subsequent interpretation. An encounter with a grizzly will likely trigger fear and flight if you spot the bear (or the bear spots you) while you're hiking alone in a wilderness, however, mere curiosity when viewing a grizzly through a protective barrier at the zoo. Only after additional information about your surroundings is collected can you engage in the appropriate response. This is referred to as perception, and it will vary from person to person as well as over time.

Same Event, Different Responses

No two individuals will perceive an event in exactly the same way. You may know someone who drives to the airport on their day off while looking forward to climbing aboard a perfectly functional airplane. They then leap out of it at 10,000 feet as a member of their skydiving club. However, a person with a phobia of flying will view the air traffic control tower, observe the planes taking off and landing, and then have a full-blown panic attack. Exact same stimuli, but opposite responses; excitement and joy versus excitement and terror. Clearly, each person has processed the information before them in completely opposite ways.

No two people will perceive something in the same way because they are never responding to absolute reality. What they are really responding to is an abstraction of reality.

Let me explain: You are not responding to these words as you read them. What you are responding to is the electrochemical translation of the words into an image in your brain. The image within your brain, not the one on this page (or in an audiobook if you are listening) is the trigger of your response.

Furthermore, the image in your brain may be quite different from the image in another person's brain. You are going to filter my words through your beliefs, which in turn have been shaped by the experiences you have had. Few people have had identical life experiences so your perception of the world will invariably differ from that of others.

I was surprised to learn this while presenting a seminar on the subject of guided imagery and the immune system. This is a subject I put to the experimental test early during my career. My reasoning to conduct research pertaining to this topic was simple. If our responses are driven by an image, it shouldn't matter whether the image is arriving via a live feed through our sensory system or is derived from our memory or imagination. It's analogous to watching a movie for the first time. Your response to the actors and action will be the same whether you're watching it during the first showing or months later as a recording. Information derived from your memory is analogous to the recorded version.

The research I conducted was designed to test the hypothesis that creating an image stemming from the imagination could evoke some of the same emotions and physiological responses that would be expected were the person actually experiencing the imagined events. More specifically, my colleagues and I embarked on a study of guided imagery to determine if it was capable of altering the progression of cancer.

Even before the study was published in the *Scandinavian Journal of Behavior Therapy* in 1988, it resulted in a large amount of media attention for it was considered one of the first studies attempting to correlate a simple behavioral intervention with the inner workings of the cancer fighting cells of the immune system.

That media attention included an interview with Diane Sawyer on the CBS television program *60 Minutes*. After the show was aired, the coverage resulted in numerous invitations from around the country to speak on this subject. As a scientist, I always make every effort to remain unbiased in order to preserve my credibility. The seminar and keynotes I presented were no exception. There was one particular keynote I remember well because two audience members heard the same words, yet interpreted them in opposite ways.

As always, I presented a balanced viewpoint, speaking about the positive aspects of imagery along with the negative. Some people believed that if a behavioral intervention could influence the progression of their cancer, then perhaps they had brought on the disease because they behaved inappropriately. They felt they were responsible for their disease, which contributed to their stress. Others took comfort believing they had become part of the negotiation of their disease outcome and thus lessening their sense of helplessness.

At the end of the program, a woman came up to me and said, "Dr. Hall, when I had cancer diagnosed, the doctors gave up on me. They said it was too advanced to respond to any of the available treatments and that I had less than two years to live. Then I read a book on imagery, which I believed in. It made sense so I tried it. Do you know that was six years ago? I know the imagery saved my life, and I want to thank you for saying all the wonderful things you just said about it."

A short time later, a man approached and introduced himself as a psychiatrist. He told me, "I've always known that guided imagery is a crock, and I just want to tell you that it was refreshing to hear a scientist who has done research in this field declare it's a waste of people's time."

Those two individuals heard the same words, spoken using the same inflection and pauses, yet each stated opposite interpretations of what I had said. One focused only on the positive data supporting her preexisting belief that imagery would help, while the other focused only on the negative data validating his preexisting belief that imagery was a waste of time.

It was then that I appreciated the wisdom of the Chinese proverb, "What the eye sees and what the ear hears is what is already in the mind." In other words, we have a tendency to create images that will validate a preexisting belief. It's analogous to an artist contemplating a beautiful scene. She sets up her easel, props up the canvas, and lays out her paints. She soon realizes there must be an airport nearby because, periodically, planes fly across the horizon. But she decides the planes don't belong in this natural setting, so even though they are part of the scene, she doesn't include them. She then becomes aware of a beautiful and well-weathered cedar tree that happens to be behind her. It's not part of the scene, however, it would add immensely to the beauty if it were. Consequently, she adds it to the foreground. It's called artistic license, and we all do it.

We have a tendency to delete those thoughts and beliefs that we do not want to be part of our image, and we include items in our image that were never a part of the original experience. In addition, the image changes over time as our memory distorts the original details. Therefore, over time the image can become a progressively less accurate abstraction of what actually happened. It is not that people are deliberately deceiving themselves or others. Instead, it seems your mind tends to operate on some sort of belief-driven autopilot.

Belief-Shaped Images

It's important to understand that the event giving rise to an emotion is not just the image, but the beliefs that transform the image into one that gives rise to an emotion. Should the belief give rise to fear, the person will take steps to reduce it. For example, they'll walk a greater distance to avoid an aggressive dog. If they experience pleasure upon spotting a friend, they'll take extra time approaching and then greeting the person.

When there's a profound discrepancy between the way you perceive events and reality, the resultant image may be so distorted, it drives inappropriate emotions along with inappropriate behaviors. In short, fear of failure driven by an inaccurate belief and subsequent image can lead to withdrawal and failure to achieve goals.

Know more and fear less. The more open-minded you are, the more you read, the more you experience, the more feedback you accept from other people, the more willing you are to listen to alternative viewpoints, then the greater the probability your image will closely reflect reality. While perception creates the image, beliefs shape that perception. That's the part you can control and change.

To determine whether your belief is appropriate for the circumstances, ask yourself the seven questions pertaining to beliefs that were introduced in chapter 5.

- Are these your beliefs or those of someone else?
- Are your beliefs based on experience?
- Can you think of times in your life when your belief was challenged by reality?
- Have your beliefs ever kept you from achieving a goal?
- Are certain themes reflected in your beliefs?
- Are you willing to change one or more of your beliefs if they are obstacles to your goals?
- Are your beliefs serving a useful purpose?

And make sure you keep asking those questions because circumstances can change. So don't just ask those questions once, and then cling to the belief because it was warranted last month. Perhaps your belief that you are not qualified to complete a project may be justified under a specific set of conditions. But those conditions can change.

For example, you can say, "I cannot build this website right now, but if I take classes on the subject, I will acquire the skills I need to achieve this objective." And remember to examine where the belief came from. Is it yours? I told you how my life has been changed by the erroneous belief that no one in my family was any good at learning math. I can only imagine the large number of people who never started pursuing their dream because they were told, "Oh, you can't possibly make a living doing that!" It was not the absence of skill, but rather the lack of initiative that turned the belief into a self-fulfilling prophecy.

Think about it. An African American girl born into poverty in a small Southern town in Mississippi, who, at the age of thirteen, experienced abuse and molestation and became a runaway teenager. What are the chances of her becoming a successful woman who reaches out and helps millions of people every day? What if Oprah Winfrey had failed to do what she knew she could?

What are the odds a college dropout would travel to Albuquerque, New Mexico, with a preposterous dream and would start his business in a cheap motel with hookers next door, and then end up one of the richest men in the world? No erroneous belief stopped Bill Gates.

Who would have thought a young woman born in Nutley, New Jersey—a former model turned caterer—would become an entrepreneur who could rival the likes of Bill Gates? Nothing, not bad advice or criticism, stopped Martha Stewart. And thank goodness, Michael Jordan did not accept his high school basketball coach's belief. The one who benched him.

Make certain you know what your beliefs are. It's the most important step. Many people don't know. Then determine if your belief is based on accurate and complete information.

Sometimes, we have a tendency to make decisions based on only a limited amount of available information. Some people value certain things so profoundly that unless a coworker subscribes to the same religious beliefs or is of the same political persuasion, they will avoid contact. They remain oblivious to the fact the individual they are avoiding has the skills to help them undertake projects that could propel them to the top of their profession.

Perhaps your neighbor has the potential of becoming a close friend, but because of one characteristic, you make no attempt to get to know him. Occasionally, your intuition pays off and you rightly reject a person based on a tiny fragment of information. More often, however, a fully informed decision will lead to greater success than a decision that is not.

Things Are Not as Bad as They Seem

Nothing will disrupt progress toward a goal more than an unexpected setback. It happens to all of us because not all circumstances fall within your control. In general, the more adversity you've experienced, the greater the likelihood you'll be able to brush yourself off and press on.

That's because as a result of having successfully overcome an obstacle, you learn that most things in life are only temporary. To quote a famous line from the Anglo-Saxon poem "Deor," roughly translated as "This, too, shall pass." A person who has experienced unexpected setbacks will also be in a position to reflect upon the previous incidents, which may well make the current episode seem trivial by comparison.

I was living in Grenada during the Marxist revolution in March of 1979 and recall dozens of panic-stricken American medical students seeking any avenue to escape the island. They even offered local fishermen vast sums of money to transport them to safety in small, dilapidated boats. Thank goodness the fishermen declined. It's unlikely many of those rickety boats would have safely made the open sea crossing to the next island.

On the other hand, the expatriates who resided on the island took it all in stride. One had experienced revolutions in Africa, while another had lived through the blitz in London during World War II. Their perspective was different. They had been through far worse and had survived. Therefore, they were confident that they would do so this time. The expatriates simply ignored the rebels as they continued with their usual routines. In actuality, the revolution was not nearly as bad as some perceived it. Except for the nightly shoot-on-sight curfew, life pretty much went on as usual.

Dwell on What You Have, Not on What You've Lost

Another strategy that will enable you to make progress in the face of obstacles is to focus on what you have and not on what you have lost.

Let's say your computer crashed less than forty-eight hours before the deadline and critical work has been lost because you forgot to back up the files. Dwelling on the lost files will make your situation worse. Fear mixed with anger will team up to send your stress and anxiety into the red zone. You'll find yourself in full-blown panic mode.

That is not the time to make any decisions about the future of the project. The files are gone, and dwelling on the loss at the end of the day isn't going to help the cause. Take a break and commit to not making any irreversible decisions, such as walking away from the project, until the next day. Get some sleep and reevaluate the situation in the morning. You probably won't get much sleep, but the worrying you'll be doing is actually a form of higher processing. You're weighing the options in your mind. Different thoughts are flying through your brain, and, who knows, perhaps some new options will emerge.

The next morning, reflect on the resources you have. Are there coworkers in a position to set aside their tasks and assist? Is there an IT department that might have some ideas about retrieving the lost files? Can you get an extension on the deadline?

Re-create in your mind an adverse experience you successfully overcame. Recall everything you did during the crisis while reminding yourself that you eventually succeeded. Remind yourself that having succeeded in the past, you can do it again.

Doing these exercises may not lead to a successful outcome; however, they will keep your focus on the project. In addition, you'll be taking steps to control your emotions and make them work for you instead of against you. By taking these steps, you'll be far more likely to succeed than if you simply feed your fear by ruminating over what's been lost. You're also exerting a measure of control over the situation, which lessens any feelings of helplessness.

Overcoming setbacks is in large part a skill you can learn, practice, and then hone to perfection. It's also important to clear your mind of any groundless beliefs that might impede success. Then replace them with new ones capable of instilling a sense of optimism. You might also project your mind in space and time to an earlier stage of life. There, you might stumble upon a long-forgotten hand-me-down belief capable of steering you in the right direction. I'm speaking from experience. My grandmother always reminded us children, "Life is like a toilet. You get out of it what you put into it." What she meant was focus on the positive, and good things will happen.

Optimism

With a stroke of her pen, my sixth-grade teacher had as great an impact on shaping my life as any adventure I embarked upon.

"Nicholas doesn't pay attention. He wastes time, and he fails to follow instructions," she wrote on the back of my report card strewn with C minuses and Ds.

Hardly words of praise, yet they instilled in me a sense of confidence and optimism. The lasting message was conveyed between the words: "Nicholas doesn't . . . wastes time . . . fails to follow instructions." It was me who was in command. My lackluster grades were not the consequence of a low IQ or some genetically inspired inability to learn. Instead, those Ds were the result of my action or rather lack of actions. At any time, I *chose* I could earn As and Bs. All I had to do was start paying attention and following instructions. That was my choice, and it required no help from anyone.

Pity the poor student who, despite paying attention and following instructions, still earned low grades. Chances are, the teacher would have concluded, John is just not good at math, or Mary just doesn't do well on tests. John and Mary will learn that they have a problem with no clear solution in hand. They are being told that there is a problem with *them*. I was told there was a problem with my *choices*. As a consequence, I came to recognize that most of life's hurdles are temporary setbacks and capable of being overcome. I learned to be optimistic.

Here are some other lessons I've learned along the way:

- Nothing in life is permanent. While lessons learned early in life can have a lasting impact, pessimism can be changed. The steps are the foundation of cognitive psychology.

- Learn to succeed through failure in the same way many successful CEOs have. Despite being labeled as dyslexic or ADHD as children, they found the problem was not their style but the mismatch with their environment.

- Optimism is realistic, not positive, thinking. It is recognizing that doing something can make a difference. It is no wonder optimism predicts a reduced incidence of cancer and improved immunity.

- Optimists have more friends since they are more fun to be around. Social support is yet another pathway to optimal health.

Clearly, optimism is a trait that can be ingrained during early childhood. However, that's water under the bridge. You can't go back and rewrite history. So what are your current options? What steps might you take to instill a sense of optimism long after having a pessimistic explanatory style imposed on your psyche? There are things you can do, but it won't be easy. That's because it may require reprogramming your brain.

In the face of adversity, you are likely to respond to a threat by engaging in either approach or avoidance behaviors. In the extreme, you would either fight or run away. Associated with the approach system is optimism for it's unlikely that you would choose to engage in a behavior unless you anticipated a positive outcome. Enthusiasm and pride would generally occur when moving toward a goal.

In contrast, another system is associated with withdrawal from an aversive environment. Negative affect, perhaps in the form of disgust or fear, will generally be associated with putting distance between you and the source of a threat, which in turn will prevent you from achieving your goal.

Psychologist Martin Seligman has conducted a number of studies revealing that a person's individual coping style will have a bearing on their response to threat. People who recognize that adversity does not have to permeate every aspect of their life and is temporary and mostly the result of external events have an optimistic explanatory style. In general, they will rebound faster from stress-inducing events and will likely view the event as a challenge while engaging in approach behaviors. Their attitude is, "I can do this."

In contrast, those who personalize events and embrace the belief that every aspect of their life will be negatively and permanently impacted are said to have a pessimistic explanatory style. They tend to view adversity as an obstacle and to engage in avoidance behaviors. It's readily apparent how this style goes hand in hand with procrastination.

Anatomy of Optimism

A specific part of the brain called the prefrontal cortex appears to be partially responsible for determining whether a person will approach or avoid a threat. This bi-lobed structure is located above the bones forming the eye sockets. Different regions of the prefrontal cortex are responsible for shaping responsiveness to events. The left side contributes to positive feelings since patients with damage to this region are more likely to be depressed. This observation is consistent with electrophysiological data. When healthy people are exposed to emotion-eliciting events, there is increased activity on the left side of the frontal lobes when the person is experiencing happiness, while there is more activity on the right side of this structure when they are sad.

So often, we tend to think that if something is associated with an event in the brain, it must be the cause of a behavior and not itself subject to behavioral influences. That is not true of the prefrontal lobes. A technique called mindfulness meditation has been shown to bring about not only a change in brain activity but also a change in outlook. It's a technique requiring instruction and practice. Therefore, it is beyond the scope of this book to provide an in-depth description of the protocol.

Nonetheless, mindfulness meditation involves the induction of a meditative state, while maintaining an awareness of something in the environment. It might be an aroma, sound, or some other feature, which, otherwise, would not be a part of your conscious awareness. This is followed by taking steps to change your outlook.

The objective is not to replace pessimism with positive thinking. That is not a feature of the optimistic explanatory style. Bad things happen, and when they do, there may be nothing to justify a rosy outlook. As defined by Seligman, optimism pertains to how you perceive adversity. It's more about non-negative thinking than it is about being positive. Seligman has formulated what he refers to as the ABC technique for replacing a pessimistic explanatory style with one that is optimistic.

A. **Adversity:** Identify the problem minus any feelings. It's merely a description of what has happened.

B. **Beliefs:** Examine the beliefs that are shaping your response.

C. **Consequences:** Reflect upon your actions along with their consequences.

This is a type of cognitive behavioral therapy, which is used extensively by mental health workers. The process is as follows:

1. Identify the automatic thoughts that make you feel worse.

2. Consider opposite interpretations as you dispute these harmful thoughts.

3. Create different explanations.

4. Develop a strategy to distract yourself from negative thoughts.

5. Examine carefully the beliefs that give rise to your pessimism and set about to replace them with optimistic ones.

Images Run the Show

Up until now, I have discussed how your beliefs can shape images triggered by events that might discourage you from proceeding toward a goal. But do you know that you can create images using nothing more than your imagination? These images require no external input. Sometimes, they can help you achieve the goals you dream of. Described next is the protocol.

Determine what your image will be. Your favorite vacation spot. A quiet room. A concert hall, beach, or garden. It can be from your past and based on fact, or it can be a conceived image using your thoughts. Or, perhaps, you'd like to create a mental collage, drifting from one pleasant place to another. If it helps, gaze upon the scene in a picture and let that be your setting, imagining you are now a part of it.

Select an object, a fragrance, or a piece of music that will be a part of your image. Make it something unusual that you would not normally encounter. This is going to be your conditioned stimulus. By having it present when you create the image, it will acquire similar properties to Pavlov's bell. You'll use it to activate the emotions and physiology associated with your imagery session. Later, just by exposing yourself to the object, you will more quickly enter the state you want to be in. Some people create a vision board or dream board—an actual poster placed in their office or personal space.

Isolate yourself from distracting, sensory stimuli. Make sure the room is quiet, that you are comfortable with no distractions. Include dimensions that will enhance your image. Appropriate music and fragrances may enrich the mood, so let them bathe your imagination.

Relax. If your mind is preoccupied with something else, intrusive thoughts will make it difficult for you to create anything except superficial images. Colors, aromas, sounds, and an awareness of small details within the place you have created will more likely occur when you are totally relaxed. Take a warm bath. Listen to relaxing music. Read some poetry. Take deep, abdominal breaths. Use progressive muscle relaxation. Do whatever works for you to induce a state of relaxation.

Immerse yourself in your journey. Picture the setting from afar, as though you are watching the scene on a large theater screen. Observe the objects, people, and colors and hear the sounds and smell the fragrances. Is your "happy place" warm or cold? Identify a place where you would like to be and move toward it. Become a part of the scene. As you take in your surroundings, gently rotate your head in a tension-releasing sweep around your shoulders, observing new things as your head slowly moves.

Practice creating images. Remember, it's your belief-driven image that governs the emotions, which, in turn, are able to impact every aspect of your personal and professional life. If you want to induce emotions that will facilitate your achievement of goals, you must learn to control the images that give rise to those emotions.

This is the process used by the world champion speed skater Dan Jansen. When faced with beliefs having the potential to interfere with an upcoming race, he would recall the moment he had won a championship. His posture, facial expression, and movements associated with winning were induced. Sports performance coach Jim

Loehr had him act like a winner to facilitate his achieving his goal. It worked prior to the 1994 Winter Olympics when he not only won a gold medal, but set a new record in the process. This is something we can all do when intrusive thoughts start to delay our progress toward a work-related or personal goal.

Earlier I described the characteristics of core, cultural, hand-me-down, advertised, and biological beliefs and the questions you should ask to determine whether the belief that guides you is the one you really should be embracing. It's important to do this before anything else, for your beliefs impact virtually every aspect of your life.

Takeaways

- You respond to mental images of events, not the event itself.
- Images are shaped by experience and beliefs.
- During times of adversity, dwell on what you have, not on what you've lost.
- Engage in realistic thinking, not positive thinking.
- Collect all the information you can to accurately perceive events.
- Circumstances are rarely as bad as they seem after the fog of emotion clears.

8

Because I Can't Do It Alone

When pursuing a goal, other people can either help or hinder your progress, but only if you let them. There are steps you can take to enlist the help of others, and things you can do when dealing with toxic personalities bent on impeding your progress.

How Good Are You in Seeking Support?

Do you believe it's a sign of weakness to ask others for help? Have you always been on your own? Do you think people will not like you if you expose your weaknesses?

Many people do not have meaningful contact with others because they have never learned how to make themselves open and vulnerable in relationships. This is not to say that it's necessary or even healthy to run to others whenever the slightest problem arises. Instead, recognize the opportunities to give and receive support from others.

Some people create personal barriers to helpful relationships. Because of unhealthy beliefs, they may intentionally avoid contact with others. You may be outgoing in the workplace where your position in the hierarchy is well-defined, but ill at ease in social settings. Perhaps the opposite applies to you. If there are circumstances under which you have difficulty communicating with others, is it due to one of the following beliefs?

- I will look silly or intrusive.
- I will be seen as making sexual overtures.
- I am unworthy to be speaking to that person.

If any of these beliefs ring true to you, apply the same questions used to probe other beliefs:

- Are these your beliefs or those of someone else?
- Are your beliefs based on experience?
- Can you think of times in your life when your belief was challenged by reality?
- Have your beliefs ever kept you from achieving a goal?
- Are certain themes reflected in your beliefs?
- Are you willing to change one or more of your beliefs if they are obstacles to your goals?
- Are your beliefs serving a useful purpose?

When you do interact with others, let them know what you need. Don't expect them to read your mind. Some people intuitively will know how to support you, while others may not. On the other hand, relationships can be a reason you never get around to doing the things you need to do.

Some people are manipulative, deceptive, or overly controlling. Such relationships—personal, professional, or otherwise—can take a serious toll on your motivation if you find yourself on the receiving end of these tactics. You'll unwittingly assist others in achieving their goals, but you'll never reach yours.

If you answer yes to any of the following questions, you need to take steps to modify your response to others.

- Have you ever purchased something that you didn't really want? The salesperson spent a lot of time explaining the features of the TV, which wasn't really what you wanted. But you bought it anyway because you didn't want her to be upset with you for having wasted her time.
- Have you ever accepted a food or beverage item when you didn't want to? You really didn't want the death by chocolate dessert but ordered one anyway since all your friends were indulging.
- Have you ever agreed to do something counter to your value system? Having a day to relax was something you were really looking forward to. However, when a neighbor asked you to babysit her daughter so she could go shopping, you said yes.
- Have you ever regretted not taking action? You witnessed someone shoplift a ring at a craft show, but said nothing to the vendor because you didn't want to get involved.

Now reflect on why you responded the way you did.
- What beliefs allowed you to be manipulated?

- What beliefs kept you from holding your ground or speaking your mind?
- If someone wanted you to do something against your will, how best would they accomplish this?

Reflecting on your answers to these questions will help you identify the problem. The next step is to seek a remedy. The rules for dealing with relationship problems are quite involved and must be tailored for each situation. Nonetheless, here are some general guidelines.

- Do what you believe is right, not what is expected.
- Your choices are always yes, no, or none of the above.
- You don't have to give a reason for your choice.
- You don't have to apologize for your choice.
- Take some time—even sleep on it before deciding.
- Watch for signs of deception.
- Recognize your vulnerability.

Why is pondering these questions important? Because if you are pursuing goals to please others, then those goals are probably not yours.

Dealing with Difficult People

Let's look at specific examples of how you might better deal with people who are keeping you from doing the things you need or want to be doing. Start by paying attention to their strategy. While the precise manner in which you deal with a person will need to be customized based on the circumstances, the general approaches suggested as follows could be used in almost any setting in which you might encounter one of the following types of individuals:

BELLIGERENT PEOPLE.

Let's begin with the belligerent supervisor who manages through intimidation. You have no idea when an outburst is going to occur, but you know from experience it will. Most important is to avoid a feeling of helplessness. Doing so will find you playing the classic role of a victim. Or if you respond by yelling back, you may have lost control of your emotions while being manipulated by the other individual.

Your job is to be rational, deal with the situation in a constructive way, and continue to be the mature person you are. A tall order when someone is verbally attacking you. Your first response may be an increase in heart and respiration rate. The latter are classic stress responses associated with anger and fear, the two emotions most likely to be elicited.

Take a deep breath, exhale slowly while reminding yourself the outburst is not about you personally but about something the other person believes you have done. Focus on what the individual is saying to determine whether there is anything useful in his outburst. If it's strictly a personal attack, then you need to end it. Here are some guidelines.

Ask the person to please stop, and very calmly inform him that you do not appreciate being treated in this manner.

You are conveying a clear and concise message, which is neither threatening nor defensive. It's also a response placing you firmly in control.

State you want a time-out. If the person is speaking so loudly that he can't hear you, place the palm of your hand over your fingers of the other hand in the same manner an athlete might to signal a time-out is being sought. That gesture, by itself, can distract the individual long enough to convey your request. Let it be known you want to learn his concerns, but that you need him to slow down. Don't ask him to calm down. This could be perceived as a criticism. However, asking him to slow down conveys that you want to hear what he has to say. This, in itself, can reduce the level of conflict

Agree with the attacker. Acknowledge the problem is serious and needs to be discussed. However, it has to be done on rational terms, not emotional terms. That message can be communicated very subtly when you say, "Let's talk about this. You start and while you are describing to me your view of the problem, I won't interrupt. When you're finished, I would like an opportunity to pose any questions I might have."

By engaging in this kind of response, you are firmly in control and are serving in the capacity of a mediator. You have assured the individual you are interested in what he has to say without interruption. This, in itself, can have an overall calming effect.

BACK STABBERS.

Some people will greet you with a smile and say some of the sweetest things in your presence, but the second you are out of sight will go out of their way to stab you in the back. Chances are such an individual has very low self-esteem and in his own mind is elevating his stature by criticizing those he perceives to be superior.

You probably are not the only victim of such a person in which case a group response may be in order. Identify others who are being manipulated in the same way. This shouldn't be too difficult because the back stabber is probably undermining them in your presence.

Initially, go along with the game and even suggest that everyone gather for a social function, such as lunch or dinner after work. Then get your colleagues to agree to state the same message. This can be done in different ways, but the message should be, "We need to improve working conditions, and this means you have to stop voicing your concerns about us to others. You need to address the problem with the person who can do something about it."

It's quite likely this type of individual will respond with all sorts of pleasant things along with excuses. He may even deny what you know to be true. It is important that during the confrontation you remain calm, maintain eye contact, interject no emotion, and simply repeat the message, "You must stop this behavior."

You may not be able to change a back stabber, because changing a person's behavior and ingrained habits is difficult. But you may convince the person you and your colleagues are not the ones who should be targeted for this type of manipulation. The consequence may be that the back stabber will move on and seek other targets. This is not ideal, but at least they're leaving you alone so you can more easily get things done and achieve your goals.

CRISIS SEEKERS.

These people seem to have an enormous amount of energy. They are extremely focused on what they do, but only when it has reached the point of a crisis. Often, the crisis they are attending to has absolutely nothing to do with what they are supposed to be doing.

How about these examples: A coworker's child has become ill, or the manager's furnace has malfunctioned. Perhaps the IT guy's car has broken down. Each of these demands the person's total attention. As a result, they're making no contribution to achieving the goal at hand. A solution might be to frame their contribution as a crisis.

For example, explain to such individuals how desperate it is that they mobilize their energy and come through for you. Interject as much drama as you can in describing how terrible the consequences will be if the job or the project is not completed on time. Be careful not to be critical. If they feel rejected or inferior, that will become their crisis. You need to be prepared to use this technique continuously.

There is nothing wrong with such individuals' basic behavior. You just want them to redirect the same overly dramatic enthusiasm and energy into helping you or the organization to stay on course.

INVALIDATORS.

Another type of person who can impede success is the invalidator. They are constantly finding things to criticize. They don't have temper tantrums, but their constant criticism eventually eats away at your self-esteem. Often, these people are perfectionists who engage in dichotomous thinking; if a single small mistake is made, then everything is wrong.

You may have spent a week or more working on a special project, which is on schedule. That's when the invalidator takes one glance at what you've accomplished and declares it's absolute trash!

That's highly doubtful. There may be some component that requires adjustment, but not the entire effort. First, get control of your breathing so your physiology doesn't cause you to lose control. Then reflect on the considerable amount of time you spent working to the best of your ability on the task. Next, sit down with the person, most likely a supervisor, and ask them to explain what part of the project is most problematic.

In this way, you're not ignoring their comment, nor are you denying the essence of their criticism. Instead, you are getting them to single out their genuine concern after which you can set about to remedy it.

OSTRACIZERS.

The final type of difficult person is one who employs ostracism to control others. They make it difficult for you to do the job that you've been assigned by failing to pass along needed information. Often, these people experience a sense of power by excluding you from the "in group" and thereby imagine they've elevated their own status.

If this type of individual is the primary source of your stress, seek a colleague you know to be cooperative. Just make certain this individual also is a member of the so-called in group and a person the ostracizer respects. Ask that person to make sure important and relevant information be passed on to you. Don't mention the fact that you are being ostracized. Why bring attention to a problem if it's not necessary? What you need is the information you are being denied. This strategy will enable you to accomplish your goal by circumventing the ostracizer.

Colleagues can be your greatest asset in progressing toward a goal, or your greatest obstacle. Chances are you can't isolate yourself from those who may be making life difficult. However, you can change your response and attitude so their tactics do not undermine your progress.

Healing Relationships

Most of us believe our friends are conduits to pleasure, a means by which to experience joy and happiness. That they are. But our relationships with others also can improve our mental and physical health and well-being. You may not think of social support as being a behavioral intervention, but that's exactly what it is.

Indeed, loneliness is almost as much a risk factor for disease as high cholesterol or smoking. Friends also can help sustain your motivation as well as assist in the pursuit of a goal.

Unfortunately, in today's plugged-in world, with email, social media, and cell phones, many of us unplug in times of stress and isolate ourselves from what is one of the most valuable resources we have: our social support.

A classic study performed by researchers at Stanford University revealed that the hormonal response of monkeys to stress varied, depending on the amount of available social support. Just contact with familiar animals significantly reduced the amount of stress-related chemicals, including those linked with memory loss, diabetes, impaired immunity, and heart disease. Not only that, but the more "friends" the monkeys had, the more robust the effect. In short, friends can be the best medicine.

It has long been known that social support promotes health in humans, perhaps via the same hormonal changes measured in the monkeys. It's known that if you are happily married, and/or have a large network of friends, you will have a greater life expectancy than single people or those who have very few friends. In fact, people who have large networks of friends have reduced risk of accidents and a lower incidence of just about all forms of illness.

Of course, some people are not highly social beings. Like Lucy in the *Peanuts* comic strip, you may say, "I love mankind; it's people I can't stand." If you are a person like Lucy, who is not a highly social being, if you truly prefer a fairly reclusive lifestyle, or if you are recently divorced and relishing the sense of freedom, don't worry! Pets can serve as a source of social support.

A field of study known as human-animal bonding has revealed that people who have pets have lower blood pressure, in general, than people who do not. And when animals are present in long-term care facilities such as nursing homes, patients tend to recover faster from surgical procedures and are more compliant about taking their medications. It was no coincidence that during the pre-vaccine days of the COVID-19 pandemic, animal shelters were emptied by people seeking pets.

We know that some people form powerful attachments to their pets that can be as strong as the emotional bond between a parent and child. Of course the benefits of having a pet may be explained more pragmatically. Perhaps the benefits are derived from the order a pet creates. Feeding the cat is a reminder to eat. Walking the dog requires the owner to exercise as well. Caring for the pet's health, such as the annual check-up, may serve as a reminder to take our own medications. Instead of saying having animals around is beneficial, we should conclude the benefit arises from engaging in the behaviors associated with having animals around.

But what if you're a solitary sort who's also allergic to many animals? Does this mean your emotions will be so deprived that you're a magnet for illness and injury? No. Odd as it may seem, caring for plants works as well. It's a tough concept to explain on the basis of love and bonding, but studies do reveal the plant connection leads to beneficial results.

Investigators at Yale University conducted studies in which plants were placed in patients' rooms. In some, the hospital staff cared for the plants. In other rooms, the patients were asked to take care of them. Those patients who tended to the plants had speedier, less complicated recoveries than those who did not.

So what do a plant, an animal, and a person all have in common? (If you recently endured a nasty divorce, you may think of several similarities.) However, in the context of explaining the health benefits, it's responsibility—responsibility for a plant, a pet, and for a loved one. We can take this one step further. Accepting responsibility for your own health is a behavioral intervention that also is conducive to a state of good health.

Emotion Disclosure

Keeping emotions pent up without expressing them can have a negative impact on your health and ability to succeed. There's an easy way to remove this potential impediment—translating emotions into words. Doing this allows you to perceive emotions from a new perspective.

The process is referred to as disclosure of emotions and can improve both your physical and mental health. For example, under well-controlled conditions, undergraduate college students were asked to recall the most traumatic event in their lives. One group narrated only the factual occurrences of the event, with no mention of their feelings about it. A second group described both the event and their feelings. A control group was asked to simply state what they were wearing at the time of the event or some other information having no emotional connotation.

Those people who recalled their feelings about the events experienced an initial episode of increased anxiety as well as a decline in their immune systems. But over the course of the semester, it was the members of the group recalling their feelings whose immune systems actually were more robust, requiring fewer visits to the student health center. There was something about the process of talking about the experience that was emotionally therapeutic and had a beneficial impact on the immune system's ability to rebound.

These results were most likely due to the students' getting it off their chest. In the context of anger, it's well established that internalizing this emotion is particularly damaging to the cardiovascular system. In addition, first responders who talk about the gruesome scenes they have witnessed can avert posttraumatic stress disorder when given the opportunity to discuss their feelings.

Other explanations have also been offered. Among the most plausible is that when speaking or writing about a problem, it forces you to slow down. Information, which has been ricocheting around the emotional brain, is delayed during its translation into language. The problem then is perceived through different sensory pathways: the eyes and the kinesthetic senses in the case of written disclosure, or the ears in the case of oral disclosure. Each form also takes time, adding a third modality. As a result, you'll find it easier to recognize solutions such as removing the perceived obstacle to getting things done. It's as though you've slipped on a pair of night-vision goggles enabling you to see what was there all along, but hidden in the darkness of despair.

Desensitization is another hypothesized possibility. Through the repetitive act of expressing your feelings, either on paper or by talking about them, the emotional edge eventually wears off. It's like watching your favorite movie over and over again. You are able to distance yourself from their impact. Realize you are tinkering with the human mind, which doesn't always respond in the way we might want it to. Rehashing a problem may fuel an emotion or become a reminder the problem is still there. However, when desensitization does work, it's likely because of one or more of the following reasons:

- Language provides a means of emotional expression.
- Language allows you to express emotions in a controllable manner.
- Translating your emotions into words allows you to perceive them from a new perspective.
- Simply altering the words you use can alter your emotional response to past or present events.

Lifelong Goals

No matter what your beliefs, ultimately, they should enable you to lead a healthier, more productive, and enriched life. But you won't succeed unless you start with the end and reflect on what it is you are seeking. Much of the discussion to this point has focused on professional goals. But just as important is taking steps to identify your personal goals as well. After all, if you don't take care of your own needs, it's unlikely you'll be of much help when called upon to meet the needs and goals of your organization.

Start by asking yourself, "What do I want out of life?" Many people live their entire lives without ever asking this essential question. As a result, their lives become a series of events dictated by external circumstances at the expense of meeting their inner needs. Unless you know what your inner desires are, you'll likely bounce from one activity to another with little choice but to accept whatever comes your way. That may not always be bad, but why not stack the odds in favor of what you define as success?

Identify your personal goals, as you did in an earlier chapter. Make them realistic and assign a time frame.

- In my lifetime, I want to _____
- Prior to retirement, I want to _____
- Before my children leave home to pursue their own goals, I want to _____
- By _____, I want to _____

Then ask yourself these questions, presented here once again:

- Are these goals attainable?
- Are they my goals or those of someone else?
- Are they stated concisely and as a positive objective?
- Am I willing to begin now? If not, under what circumstances will I begin?

- Am I willing to make changes in my life to achieve my goals?
- Are my goals consistent with my beliefs and values?
- Do any of my goals conflict with others?
- What am I willing to give up to achieve my goal?

Life is not a dress rehearsal. Live each moment as though it is your last, but assume it will go on forever. And make sure those moments are consistent with your beliefs. I suggested you complete some incomplete statements to assist in identifying your beliefs. Here's how I would complete them.

People are inherently good, but not without imperfections. Judge yourself and others in their entirety, not on the basis of one or two attributes. And be forgiving. We all make mistakes.

Stress is a natural part of life. It is a stimulus for growth. But make certain you allow time to recover, which is when the stress-stimulated growth actually occurs.

Relationships are always changing. We change constantly and need to prepare for times when the relationship may be more or less than what it was during an earlier phase.

It would be a better place to live if people adopted a very simple philosophy espoused by Rotary International, an organization committed to serving others. It's called the four-way test and is a good starting point as you consider the decisions you will make, what you will say, and what you will do.

- Is it the truth?
- Is it fair to all concerned?
- Will it build goodwill and better friendships?
- Will it be beneficial to all concerned?

And in completing the final statement, *I am* a husband and father. A son and brother. A scientist and friend. Include all the roles you play in life as you answer important questions, "Who am I?" and "What do I want?"

Takeaways

- Social support is a highly effective means by which to better cope with stress.
- Some relationships can be toxic. Learn to recognize and deal with difficult people.
- Disclosing instead of internalizing emotions can be highly effective when dealing with adversity.
- Strive to live a life with no regrets.

9

Because I Don't Have Time

At the outset, I emphasized that procrastination is an emotion-management problem, not a time-management issue. However, that doesn't mean taking steps to better manage your time is not worthwhile. It certainly is because the more efficiently you use it, the sooner you'll reach your goal.

Regrettably, I have difficulty doing this because I suffer from a malady that keeps me in a constant state of turmoil. You probably have experienced it as well. It's called optimistic bias and is characterized by the belief that you can accomplish more than is humanly possible in a given amount of time. If you suffer from this condition, here are some actions you might try.

A Six-Step Guide to Success

Many books have been written on the subject of how to better manage time, and numerous seminars provide useful tips. In general, the advice is basically the same: you need to identify the goal, break it down into its smaller and more manageable parts, then define measurable outcomes to assess your progress.

Using this process is particularly useful when pursuing a short-term goal such as a time-sensitive work-related project. However, there are other types of goals that may take years or decades to achieve. They are the ones that may add meaning to your life, but can be derailed by the same factors that lead to procrastination in the workplace.

Everyone needs to have objectives that they want to achieve in order to give their life purpose. Whatever the dream happens to be, it has to be realistic and something you truly want—not something you are doing just to please other people.

Did you know that just thinking about a goal or writing that goal down will help facilitate your accomplishing it? Once you've identified what it is you want to achieve, it becomes easier to identify the information and circumstances that will help you achieve that goal.

Here are the six steps to success:

1. **Divide projects into manageable components**. Break your goal into smaller and more manageable parts. The reason is quite simple. When you focus on the end, the undertaking may appear overwhelming. If you want to write a book, for example, it may be very difficult getting the motivation to begin because you feel that you couldn't possibly accomplish such a goal.

But no one has ever written a book. Instead, people write words, which come together as sentences, which form paragraphs and then chapters. It's also a way to organize your time in the most efficient manner possible.

2. **Avoid setting time limits.** Most of the time, I recommend that you set a time during which you need to accomplish a particular goal. It might be within a certain number of days, weeks, or, perhaps, months. Setting deadlines provides structure. Be careful, though. If you fail to accomplish your goal within that defined time frame, you may end up reinforcing your belief that you are a failure. Set the goal, but impose a time limit only if it is needed to help you maintain focus. Sometimes, it doesn't really matter when you complete the task. Whether your goal is to lose weight or to create a piece of art, you are still a success as long as you are making progress. This strategy won't work when responding to the demands of your boss, but if there's no need to impose a time constraint, then why add to your anxiety?

3. **Don't overpublicize your goal.** Some professionals recommend that you tell others about your objectives to provide the additional motivation you might need in order to see the task through to completion. Of course, you should share your goal with those who will be affected by it. Furthermore, many people benefit by having a buddy with the same goal. How-

ever, I'm advising against making prominent, public announcements.

Why set yourself up for embarrassment if you fail to accomplish your objective? It's just not necessary. In fact, it may encourage others to badger you. Instead of subjecting yourself to public scrutiny, go about achieving your goal and wait for others to notice. That's a much better way to do it.

4. **Deal with beliefs.** If you are a person who sets a goal, but you never seem to accomplish it, consider the possibility that the reason is not because you don't have the necessary skills to organize your time. Instead, you may be encountering some hand-me-down beliefs. If a parent or other authority figure instills negative beliefs at an impressionable age, those beliefs can easily become self-fulfilling prophesies. Furthermore, beliefs about yourself don't change overnight. Sometimes, the most important first step in achieving a particular objective is to change the way you see yourself and to start believing that you do have the ability to achieve your dreams.

5. **Do it for yourself.** Make sure the goal you set is truly your goal and that what you're doing is not intended to just please someone else. It might please others, but that should not be the primary motivation. I've lost track of the number of medical students I've taught who didn't want to be doctors. They were struggling to get good grades and to achieve that objective

because it wasn't what they wanted. It's what their parents wanted. They would reach a certain point in their training and realize they were not pursuing their own dream, but someone else's. After having invested, maybe, ten years of their life in achieving this goal, they felt stuck with no alternative but to complete it. Recently, a former student who is now a successful doctor contacted me about how to start a new profession as a motivational speaker. Despite all the external trappings of success, he was unable to enjoy life because his goals were inconsistent with his values. Alternatively, you might select a particular goal to impress a specific group of people. Ironically, those people may not be the least bit concerned about your personal happiness. In the process, you sacrifice your own development as a person.

6. **Be flexible.** When setting about to pursue a dream, be flexible. If you have set lifelong goals, then you need to review these at least once a year to see if the goals you felt were important when you were in your twenties are still important when in your forties. You may have new responsibilities, health problems, or face other circumstances that limit what is realistic for you to accomplish. So, on a regular basis, subject your goals to reassessment in much the same way that you should subject your beliefs to reanalysis. Answer these questions:

   • Are your goals new, or did you formulate them years ago but have yet to achieve them? If the latter, why have you been unable to make more headway?

- Do you have too many goals and insufficient time to spend working toward them?
- Have you wasted time and effort on objectives that had nothing to do with your lifelong goals?
- Are your values mirrored in the steps you take to achieve your objectives?

Reflecting on the answers to these questions will shed considerable light on the changes you might need to make in order to begin making progress. If you don't remove hidden obstacles, making progress can be discouragingly slow.

What's Your Optimal Time?

You may have a surplus of energy, but you may not have it at the times you need it. Many people make the mistake of tackling the tasks that they have to do on the basis of urgency. They fail to take into account that there are times of the day when they are better able to take on certain types of tasks as opposed to others.

I'm sure you have heard others declare "I'm a morning person" or "I'm a night owl." As the sun progresses from the eastern horizon to the west, so are our bodies changing. When you awaken in the morning, you have coursing through your veins a large amount cortisol, a hormone that helps to mobilize energy. As the day progresses, the levels gradually drop, bottoming out at about

3:00 in the morning when most people are asleep. It then rises when exposed to sunlight and while moving about in the morning, thereby providing the energy you need to make it through the day. This natural cycle is called a circadian rhythm. There are also ultradian rhythms. As opposed to a circadian rhythm, which means about the day, ultradian rhythms mean within the day. One of the best characterizations is the constant shifting in brain dominance between the left and right hemispheres every 90 to 120 minutes.

You've undoubtedly heard of the left brain versus the right brain. (Not to be confused with the left versus right prefrontal lobes discussed earlier.) Regions in the left-brain hemisphere are primarily responsible for language and analytical skills. Those in the right brain hemisphere, however, are involved more with artistic pursuits. For example, creating sculptures, music awareness, and music expression depend upon neurons based in the right hemisphere. Every 90 to 120 minutes, you switch. For part of the day, the electrical activity on one side of the brain is more pronounced than it is on the other.

For example, have you ever found yourself in the middle of a task, where you are in what psychologists would refer to as flow or, in athletics, the zone? You are doing what you need to do almost effortlessly, and it seems as though you could go on forever. Your performance is flawless. The clay is literally coming to life in your hands as you create the piece of art.

But then, after a short break, you return to the task and the clay crumbles in your hands. You just can't seem to regain the focus you had previously. Or the report you had been writing with little effort now is impossible to resume when you return to the task. A contributing factor could very well be that you have switched from the side of the brain that would facilitate accomplishing this task. Writing a report depends on language. That's a left-brain function, while creating a sculpture would require the right.

What you need to do is select the time of day when you are most likely to be able to complete the task at hand. If it requires a certain amount of energy and physical exertion, then select a time of day when your glucocorticoids will be elevated—for example, the morning. If it's a language-based task, then select a time of day when you are more likely to be in your left hemisphere as opposed to your right.

No, you do not need sophisticated brain-wave measuring machines to determine which side of the brain is most active. You may be able to determine this by performing the following nasal exercise.

Take a deep breath in through your nose. Now do it again, and pay attention through which nostril you are breathing. Obviously, you are probably breathing through both simultaneously, but if you pay very careful attention, you'll notice the air is passing more readily through one side as opposed to the other. What facilitates the passage of air is constriction (narrowing) of blood vessels on that side. The more constricted the blood vessels, the more readily air will pass through the corresponding nostril. It turns out the nerves that regulate blood vessels do not cross over to the opposite side of the body like other nerves. That means when the blood vessels are constricted on the left side of your body (and nose), they are constricted on the left side of your brain. It is hypothesized that when the diameter or opening in the blood vessel is reduced by constriction, there is less blood flow on that side. Blood is still flowing, but is slightly reduced.

The scientists who have conducted this research believe that it means you also have slightly less brain activity on the constricted (easier to breath) side and more on the opposite side with more blood flow. Blood transports oxygen and glucose, along with the nutrients required to manufacture a myriad of essential brain chemicals, so it sort of makes sense.

What is the translation of this information? Your brain is slightly less active on the same side of the brain as the nostril with more constricted blood vessels. You can also think of it as you're operating better on the side with the stuffy nostril. It's known that the involved nerves vary their activity every 90 to 120 minutes. This is known as an ultradian rhythm and explains why the ease of breathing switches from one side to the other throughout the day. It also explains why different types of tasks such as language (left brain) versus music awareness (right brain) are more easily carried out at different times of the day.

It's 10:00 a.m. At 11:00 a.m., you have to have a critical report on your supervisor's desk. You have just switched over, and you are now breathing through your left nostril, which means, of course, that you are in your right brain. This is not the best side of the brain to be in if you want to achieve flow while writing a report. You need to be in your left brain, which is where language is based; and that, in turn, means that you should be breathing more readily through your right nostril.

Some people claim to be able to shift their dominance by forcing themselves to breathe through the nostril that they need to be breathing through. By holding your nostril and forcing yourself to breathe through one or the other, some people claim they can shift the dominance profile. A few published studies document that this can be achieved. Whether it will work for you is something that you will have to find out. It's worth a try with no downside.

I realize that all this may sound like hocus pocus. Indeed, I have to admit a certain amount of skepticism myself. However, that pertains to the explanation, not the phenomenon. You cannot dispute data, just their interpretation. A number of studies have documented that the switch from the left side to the right does indeed occur. Whether it is due to subtle changes in vasoconstriction is not absolutely clear although the explanation I've offered is reasonable. If you're a skeptic, let it go. What's important in the context of finishing what you started is the fact you now have a simple way to find out if this is a strategy you should put to use.

Regardless of the mechanism whereby the switch is taking place, the fact that changes in the brain occur has been known since antiquity in India. Hunters recognized that there were certain times during the day when they were less likely to be successful as compared with others. They determined when that optimal time of day was on the basis of which nostril they were breathing through.

Takeaways

- Divide complex tasks into smaller, more manageable components.
- Avoid overpublicizing personal goals.
- Establish personal goals based on your needs, not on those of others.
- Anticipate and plan for setbacks.
- Determine your optimal time for tackling projects.

10

Because I Don't Have Enough Energy

Unless you have sufficient energy, you'll lack both the will and the ability to achieve goals. Failure to get a good night's sleep is invariably the problem, and it's a costly one. Indeed, the sleep debt in the United States makes the economic debt look trivial by comparison.

Over 40 million Americans suffer from sleep disorders. More than 200,000 traffic accidents occur each year because of driver fatigue, and lack of sleep is the cause of 33 percent of fatal truck accidents. Studies at Stanford University have revealed that drowsy drivers are actually more impaired than most drunk drivers.

All totaled, the American Safety Council estimates that in the United States the annual financial toll due to lost productivity resulting from sleep deprivation and fatigue is approximately $136 billion. Indeed, it's time to start viewing chronic, insufficient rest as a physical disability. It's imperative that you take steps to deal with it. If you don't, you won't be able to achieve goals not because you won't but because you simply can't.

The Top Causes of Fatigue

- Too much work and not enough recreation
- Iron deficiency
- Sleep apnea
- Depression
- Emotional loss
- Thyroid problems
- Recent illness
- Snoring partners
- Sedentary behavior

The Solution

There is also a serious problem in that most people's circadian rhythms run faster than society's clocks. Many internal, biological clocks are on a twenty-six-hour cycle, while the world operates on a twenty-four-hour day.

You can, however, reset your internal clock. Expose yourself to sunlight as soon as possible after rising. Light signals the brain to synchronize most of the body's biological clocks. If you suspect a medical cause for fatigue, then guidance from a healthcare professional is clearly warranted; otherwise, consider doing some of the following activities:

Get low-impact exercise early in the day. It stimulates blood flow to your brain and elsewhere plus sets in motion a series of physiological events that enhance your ability to perform throughout the day.

Get out of bed if you haven't fallen asleep within twenty minutes. Lying there worrying about not being able to sleep only protracts the problem. Do something that's monotonous. C-SPAN and local government-access TV channels are excellent to watch, or read one of those dry trade journals you've brought home from work.

Relax. Use progressive muscle relaxation exercises, deep breathing, or simply count sheep. By concentrating on such efforts, you block troublesome thoughts, which can keep you awake.

Drink a glass of warm milk. Yes, mother was right. We now know why. Milk contains an amino acid called tryptophan, which creates a chemical chain reaction in the brain that helps induce sleep. But if you suffer from indigestion or acid reflux, milk can actually intensify such gastric discomforts. Experiment to see if this is an option for you.

Watch what you eat. Fatigue may be due to eating the wrong foods. Studies have shown that approximately two hours after consuming a meal rich in carbohydrates, you will experience fatigue as well as impaired performance on tests requiring speed and concentration. That's because the consumption of carbohydrates facilitates the transport of tryptophan into the brain. The more tryptophan that gets into the brain, the more there is available to be converted into serotonin, a neurotransmitter that stimulates sleep. Timing is everything. Save carbohydrates for dinner, not for the lunch you might consume prior to tackling a time-sensitive goal.

Get something hot. There are health benefits associated with ingesting hot peppers and sauces that contain capsaicin. This is the common ingredient capable of imparting the spicy flavor. But don't have a snack with Tabasco sauce just before you go to bed; it may trigger indigestion. That might be what's waking you up in the middle of the night.

Smoking cigarettes can disrupt your sleep cycle. Carbon monoxide in tobacco smoke, can interfere with the ability of red blood cells to transport oxygen throughout the body. The less oxygen you have, the less energy you're going to have. Smoking also can impede blood flow and the transport of oxygen by triggering the accumulation of mucus in both the windpipe and the bronchial tubes. This, in turn, will reduce the oxygenation of cells in the body. You must have adequate oxygen to convert food into energy.

Avoid caffeine and be aware there is as much caffeine in a can of cola as there is in half an average cup of coffee. Perhaps you were able to get away with drinking huge amounts of caffeinated beverages when you were younger. But as you age and your metabolism slows, it's going to take longer for the body to convert the caffeine into its inactive metabolites. Therefore, the caffeine will remain in your system for a longer period of time. Just because you were able to drink large amounts of coffee as a student, don't be surprised if those old habits are associated with some undesirable consequences later in life.

Stay away from sleeping pills. Benzodiazepines and barbiturates are addictive, and eventually you'll have no choice but to take these medications if you're going to get any sleep at all. Use them only if your doctor is convinced you have no other options. You also should avoid nightcaps. One national survey reported that 29 percent of people who say they have difficulty sleeping rely on alcohol in order to induce a state of relaxation. There's no question that alcohol will induce a state of sleep, but the quality of the sleep you get is reduced, and it's almost guaranteed you will be prone to waking up despite being exhausted. Alcohol also can impair your ability to take in oxygen. It causes overrelaxation of the muscles and inhibits the respiratory system. The net result is a reduction in your ability to breathe efficiently. All of these behaviors reduce levels of energy.

Create a diversion. There are lots of ways to divert yourself, so find a technique you feel comfortable with and use it. Whatever you do, do it vividly. If you are counting sheep, then visualize each sheep in your mind in order to block intrusive thoughts. Concentrate on your body relaxing, and chances are you won't even recall what number you got to before you fell asleep. You also can count your blessings, adding a sense of joy or gratitude to your relaxation.

Worry. There is nothing wrong with healthy worrying. It's a process whereby we weigh the options in advance of making a decision. It's when the worrying interferes with sleep or important tasks that it becomes an impediment to progress. Set aside time to worry before bedtime and get it out of your system. And don't do your worrying in bed or in your favorite chair or else they may acquire the ability to trigger worrying, just as Pavlov's bell triggered salivation in dogs.

Turn the clock. Don't have your clock staring at you next to the bed. If every time you open your eyes, you're aware of how late it is and the fact you are still wide awake, you'll continue to have trouble sleeping. Turn the clock (and your smartphone) so you at least have to expend some effort in order to see what time it is.

Cool down. What enables you to fall asleep is a subtle drop in body temperature. You can fool your body into activating processes that lower your temperature by jumping into a hot tub or taking a hot bath about an hour before you are ready for bed. The brain will be fooled into thinking you are in danger of dying from hyperthermia. Consequently, it will initiate processes designed to lower your body temperature sufficiently to compensate for the extra heat. When you leave the source of heat, those processes continue to work for a short time, so your body temperature may actually drop below normal. You'll have to experiment to determine exactly how far in advance you need to do this. Exercise also will work. When you exercise, you temporarily increase your core body temperature. Just make certain that you work out early in the evening so that your body has a chance to cool down and to enter into that overcompensation stage at the time you want to sleep.

Exercise. If you are a man in your fifties, you might be waking in the middle of the night to go to the bathroom. As men age, the prostate gland can swell and partially block the urethra. This triggers the need for frequent urination. Obviously, if you cut back on fluid intake before going to bed, this will help. However, a small amount of light exercise an hour before bedtime will work as well. Don't do anything aerobic, simply some easy stretching exercises or a short five-minute walk. This will stimulate the circulation through the kidneys thereby prompting you to get rid of a little more fluid before you go to bed.

Establish a sleep pattern and make sure you stay with it. Sleep is one of the easiest habits to condition in humans. If you train your body to fall asleep at a consistent time, then that time of day will become a conditioned stimulus.

Caution: Sleep disorders and fatigue may be secondary to an illness that cannot be regulated through behavior or supplements. For that reason, it is important to have a thorough physical examination to rule out a potentially serious medical condition.

Maintaining Energy

Even after a restful night's sleep, you still need to maintain your energy at a level sufficient to accomplish your goals for the day. That's best done with the right food. Since food is the fuel of the body, you'd think that with more, you'd be able to go further and last longer. To a certain extent, that is true. The average person needs between about 1,500 and 2,000 calories per day to make it through the workday. However, more is less important than type and time when it comes to having energy.

Lack of energy will erode your motivation and prevent you from doing what you want or need to do. Ask an athlete about hitting the wall or bonking. These expressions refer to the almost total collapse of the body, usually at a point midway through an endurance event. When blood sugar drops, the athlete's energy level bottoms out. It can happen to anyone, though. If you eat too much or too little, at the wrong time of day, or in the wrong proportions of protein, carbohydrate, and fat, your ability to perform will be significantly curtailed.

Endurance athletes use many of the following tips. If the guidelines work for people who push their physical limits for hours on end, imagine what they could do for you during the average day.

GRAZE.

Instead of eating three square meals a day, as prescribed by our culture, eat five or six meals of roughly 200 to 300 calories each. When you eat a larger amount especially of carbohydrates, the extra calories will trigger a surge of insulin in order to place the excess energy into storage.

That alone is not a problem, but it becomes one when you consume large numbers of calories, especially in the form of a high glycemic index food such as rice. Because these foods are more rapidly converted into blood sugar, the rise is quite abrupt. This, in turn, prompts the pancreas to produce a bit too much insulin, causing more sugar than intended to go into storage.

Remember the sluggish feeling you may have experienced after a big meal? Now you know why. Another way to trigger excess insulin and the same drop in blood sugar is to eat a pure sugar-laden candy bar.

While not a guaranteed solution, a good place to start is by spreading the calories you need over six smaller meals instead of the traditional three. Now your blood sugar will be more constant during the day since you're blunting the insulin response that can be followed by a slump.

CONSUME ADEQUATE PROTEIN.

The more muscle you have, the more calories you burn without doing anything. That's one of the reasons people who are lean and have lots of muscle can get away with eating large portions without gaining excess weight. Building muscle requires adequate protein in your diet.

There's considerable information about the amount of protein you should consume and it varies depending on the type of exercise you undertake. The Academy of Nutrition and Dietetics recommends the average adult consume 0.8 grams of protein per kilogram of body weight. However, the recommended amount can be as high as 1.7 grams per kilogram for high-intensity endurance athletes.

You need protein for everything from building muscle to the synthesis of immune system antibodies. Many brain chemicals are also made from the amino acids you get from protein. Foods such as milk, soy, poultry, and fish are some good sources of protein. The essential role protein plays in keeping the body running smoothly is the reason I always take high-protein energy bars with me during cross-country bicycle rides or weeklong kayak races. I also take foods high in carbohydrates when I need a quick energy boost.

But don't forget to include foods rich in vitamins and minerals. These are needed in chemical reactions that enable the food you eat to be converted into forms capable of fueling cells.

KNOW YOUR CARBOHYDRATES.

Carbohydrates contain 4 calories per gram and are the main energy source for the body. Some carbohydrates, such as refined sugar found in many soft drinks, are rapidly absorbed into the bloodstream. Other sources with varying absorption rates include baked potato, pasta, and bread. Depending on the circumstances, you may need a quick fix or one that's more sustained. Needless to say, you have options to meet your specific needs.

CONSUME ADEQUATE FIBER.

Because the human gastrointestinal (GI) tract cannot digest fiber, it does not contribute calories and is passed as waste. Fiber is, nonetheless, vital to good health. Inadequate dietary fiber leads to a sluggish GI tract, water retention, bloating, constipation, and an increased risk of developing colon cancer. In addition to containing vitamins, minerals, and antioxidants, fruits and leafy vegetables are excellent fiber sources. That's why most registered dietitians recommend consuming at least five servings per day.

In addition, the healthy bacteria residing in your gut can convert fiber into forms that can improve your mood, impact your appetite, and even influence inflammatory processes. More and more is being learned as scientists identify the varied roles these long-overlooked bacteria play.

EAT A LOW-FAT DIET.

Fats contain 9 calories per gram, more than twice the amount found in carbohydrates and proteins. In addition, the consumption of saturated fats derived from animal sources has been shown to contribute to the development of cardiovascular disease. For health reasons, saturated fats should be limited to less than 20 percent of total consumed calories.

DRINK ADEQUATE AMOUNTS OF WATER.

Many nutritionists recommend that physically active individuals consume a minimum of one gallon of water per day, although that will vary depending on your level of activity and the weather. Water aids the liver and kidneys in the detoxification of poisons and in the elimination of wastes from the body. Without sufficient water, we become dehydrated, and our organs (including muscle, liver, and kidneys) do not function optimally.

In addition, water is both an appetite suppressant as well as an excellent diuretic. Not only will high fluid intake increase urination, it also will decrease overall water retention. Although you may have to work up to a gallon a day, you will reap the benefits of your efforts almost immediately.

In fact, drinking water colder than your body temperature can actually help you to lose weight. Did you know that consuming water chilled to 40 degrees Fahrenheit can cause your body to liberate a significant number of additional calories? What an easy way to burn excess fat!

AVOID THIRST.

Proper hydration leads to enhanced thermoregulation and improved oxygen exchange in the lungs. Simply stated, the well-hydrated individual will have greater endurance and a more comfortable workout. It can also facilitate your performance in the workplace and your ability to meet deadlines. Since you do not feel thirsty until you are already in a dehydrated state, it's best to drink water with sufficient frequency to prevent the sensation of thirst.

ELIMINATE ALCOHOL.

Alcohol is not in the same category as other nutrients, but it is widely consumed so warrants mention. Alcohol is the enemy of the dieter and the athlete. It contains 7 calories per gram, nearly as much as fat, but lacks nutritional value. That means you're getting no vitamins or minerals essential for the efficient utilization of potential energy. Not only does alcohol contribute empty calories, it slows the body's metabolic rate so fewer calories are burned over time. In addition, alcohol consumption leads to a transient hypoglycemic state and subsequent food cravings. Finally, alcohol is hepatotoxic, and even moderate drinking can result in fatty deposits on the liver. None of this is good.

KEEP TRACK.

Use a book or other guide to keep track of your total calorie consumption as well as your intake of carbohydrates, protein, and fat. You should measure your food (with a measuring cup or scale) until you have a good idea of exactly what a portion actually represents. Most people overestimate portion size and, hence, underestimate their caloric intake. Some of the best resources are those published by the Academy of Nutrition and Dietetics.

Takeaways

- Optimize your sleep.
- Worrying is part of planning. It's only a detriment when it interferes with sleep and other necessary endeavors.
- Develop habits that help you fall asleep faster and enable you to awaken in a well-rested state.
- Adopt a varied and wholesome diet to maximize your energy stores.
- Stay sufficiently hydrated to avoid the sensation of thirst.
- Follow the recommendations of the Academy of Nutrition and Dietetics when considering new nutritional strategies.

11

Because It Won't Make
Any Difference

Several years ago, I learned of a study that involved a procedure considered immoral and even illegal in many societies. That's because it embraced assisted suicide. However, the healthcare provider did not administer the medication. Instead, the drug was made accessible with instructions on what to do if the patient wanted to end the dying process. The patient was always in complete control and could proceed or stop at any point.

The one thing the chaplains who coordinated the study shared in common was ministering to people who were dying. Many were hospital chaplains or worked for hospice organizations.

When I expressed surprise that members of the clergy would engage in a practice that struck me as being counter to their theology, they quickly pointed out it was entirely consistent. Their unanimous response was that if a person is ever in need of spiritual resources, it is when they are making the final transition from life to death. They were going to provide the resources and support so the patient had the option of ending their pain and suffering. One clergy person explained how she and the others were essentially working in partnership with and not against the wishes of a higher power.

As it turned out, none of the patients who were provided with the means, chose to take the final step by ending their life. It seems they weren't afraid of being dead. They were fearful of the process of dying. "Will I lose control?" "Will I be in excruciating pain?" "Will I be a burden to my loved ones?" Knowing they were in control right up until their dying breath was all it took to enable over a dozen patients to deal with the nerve-racking experience.

If being in control can help a person overcome the fear of dying, can you imagine what benefits it could provide in lesser circumstances such as the fear of failure when undertaking an important assignment?

Take Control Over Your Life

By posing questions and examining your beliefs, you have begun to take control. However, some people believe they have no choice but to relinquish control to others, especially if they are under duress. They become embroiled in an altercation with their supervisor and then assume, "There's nothing I can do. If I say anything or do anything, it won't make any difference, and I'll probably lose my job." They believe they are helpless. This can wreak havoc upon the body. A very important belief to have is that you can do something. I'll briefly review three studies to illustrate just what I mean.

First, experiments have revealed that when animals are stressed, if they are able to press a bar and turn the stressor off, this control will offset some of the health problems that would arise if they lacked this control. In short, it is not the stressor that causes the health problems, but the belief that they have no control over it, like the terminal patients I described who received control over their dying process.

Second, if the animals have had control, and then the bar is disconnected, they still do better than animals that never had control. This is because they believe things are still better. They still get shocked after pressing the bar, but based on the previous experience, they perceive things are not as bad.

Third, a group of animals was given ten shocks an hour. The day before, half had received twenty shocks, and half had received just one. Who suffered the most, even though the stressor is now identical for both groups? It was the group that previously received just one shock. Why? Because going from twenty shocks to ten instills a sense of optimism that things are getting better, while those animals that went from one shock to ten have nothing to be optimistic about; for them, things are getting worse.

These, and other related studies, suggest that the belief we are in control, coupled with the belief that things are improving, are sufficient to not only lessen the stress response, but to reduce the probability of developing stress-related illnesses. However, be careful with this concept of control. Too much control can be just as detrimental to your health as too little.

This was revealed through studies in Vietnam. Investigators found that it was middle-level officers making decisions affecting the lives of men under their command who suffered most from the effects of stress. Less so was the stress experienced by those troops who simply followed orders and went out on patrol. Therefore, having too much control and responsibility also can be detrimental to your health.

However, being completely helpless is also a serious problem. That is why I strongly recommend you always do something in a stressful situation, even if the probability of a positive outcome is remote. What is important is to avoid behaving like a victim. So often when a person is in the midst of an altercation, especially in the workplace, they will shrug their shoulders, walk away from the problem, and adopt this attitude: "There's nothing I can do. If I say or do anything, I might lose my job." So they walk down to the coffee maker and talk about their boss behind his back. If that's all you do, it's going to be extremely detrimental to your health.

When you walk away with the attitude there is nothing you can do, you are behaving like a victim, thereby making your belief a self-fulfilling prophecy. If all you do is talk about the person, you will fuel your emotion without addressing the problem that gave rise to it. Ultimately, it will be detrimental not only to the person you are talking about, but to yourself as well.

While it's okay to talk about the situation, it's preferable to do so with the person who has triggered your response. It may turn out that doing nothing is the best thing to do. But if you do nothing, make sure it is because you chose inaction as one of several options. Don't do nothing because you believe your hands are tied and there are no other choices.

Yet this course of inaction is not always as simple as it may seem. The fact is one size does not fit all. Some people believe that they must have complete control and responsibility over as many things in their environment as possible. Instead of delegating some of the workload, they try to complete the project without seeking assistance. And then there are other people who believe that it is best for someone else to do it all.

There is nothing wrong with either belief. Problems arise when people who want responsibility and control are in situations in which neither is practical. Or when a person who feels more comfortable having someone else make the decisions is suddenly put in the driver's seat. The problem is a mismatch between the person's belief about control and their environment.

Additional conflict may arise because people change. You are not the same person under stress that you are when all is calm. Under pressure, you may become just the opposite of who you usually are. Most of the time, people will adhere to the belief they formed in their family unit. If they were encouraged to be inquisitive, or to argue, that's probably the way they'll be throughout adulthood. If they were encouraged to remain silent and not speak up, that will be their tendency. Then a person might seek work environments where there's a match between the way they are comfortable responding and their supervisor's expectations.

Under stress, however, the rules change. The same people who want control during times of calm may become acquiescing or accommodating under stress. On the other hand, people who have been accommodators will now suddenly seize the reins of control. But because this type of response is not one they are accustomed to, the lack of familiarity may give rise to yet another source of interpersonal conflict. Clearly, the variable of control is not a simple one.

Actually, I'm not even sure if control itself should always be the objective. Perhaps it should be viewed as a process for achieving closure. You are more likely to experience closure when you are in control; however, it can also come about when control is granted to someone else. As long as the person abdicating control is comfortable with the arrangement.

There are occasions when a person cannot fully control their medical circumstances, but they trust their doctor or other healthcare provider. The belief that the doctor is in control and will make the right decision can be just as effective in bringing about closure.

So can a belief in a higher power. Believing that what is happening is part of some large, unified plan that ultimately will result in a beneficial outcome can bring comfort to a person experiencing duress. You don't have to know what that outcome will be, or what direction things are going to go. Simply by embracing the belief that what is happening is part of a divine plan can help some people deal with emotional turmoil.

When All Else Fails

Sometimes you simply can't control circumstances. The environment might have failed so rapidly there's nothing you can do about it. In addition, you may have limited control over your physiological and behavioral responses. You may be paralyzed with fear. However, there is always one thing you have control over right up until your final dying breath; your attitude, which no one can take away from you.

I have a good friend whose life was saved because of his attitude. In the late 1960s, Phil was in Vietnam as part of a special military unit that was ambushed by enemy soldiers. Everyone in the unit was killed, except Phil, who should have died. He was hit thirteen times with bullets from AK-47 assault rifles. Yet he survived against all medical odds. I once asked him what he attributed his survival to? Why was he able to overcome seemingly insurmountable medical odds?

He told me, "While I was lying in the jungle unable to move, feeling the life drain out of me, I was determined to stay awake. When the enemy came to slit my throat or put a bullet in my head, I wanted to spit in their faces so they would know I was dying on my terms and not theirs."

It turned out all the enemy soldiers had been killed or incapacitated. There was no one left to slit his throat, yet pure determination kept him awake until, eventually, an evacuation helicopter arrived.

Viktor Frankl was once asked why he survived the hardships of a Nazi concentration camp when so many others didn't. His answer was eloquent in its simplicity: "The belief that one day I would be asked that question." This famous psychiatrist was able to see beyond the barbed wire, remaining optimistic there would be life after his incarceration.

In addition, he seized control over those things he could influence in the bleak surroundings. There was much he wasn't able to control, but by ritualizing the act of brushing his teeth and by making a big production of getting dressed, he seized control over the small tasks he was able to influence. He never surrendered his spirit to a feeling of total helplessness.

No one sprinkles you with magical dust to induce a belief you can't do something. No one presses a button on the side of your head that induces an emotion. These are your responses, and no one else can ever control them. Ultimately the very belief that you are in control may enable you to endure one of the greatest fears we have in Western society, which is the fear of dying.

Personality and Goals

I'm sure that you've heard of the so-called Type A personality. It's the person who is always in a hurry, speaks rapidly, and often finishes your sentences because he gets impatient waiting for you to finish saying whatever it is you're going to say. It's also a person who rarely takes time to smell the roses.

There is a certain amount of overlap between the Type A personality and what is referred to as the controlling personality. This person is basically in a win/lose mode. "I'm going to win; you're going to lose. We are going to do it my way, or we are not going to do it at all." This person is personally threatened by dialogue. If you disagree with him, he'll take it as a personal affront. "Why waste time talking about the problem? We're going to do it my way, anyway, so let's just get on with it."

You've probably heard that it is the time-oriented, controlling personality who is most likely to succumb to a heart attack. Well, that's only partially correct. That was the initial interpretation of the data from the Framingham heart study when first completed. And on the basis of the limited information available to the investigators at that time, it was a correct interpretation.

Subsequently, other scientists designed more expansive studies. It turns out there was something else that accounted for most of the correlation between the Type A personality and coronary arterial disease. Anger and hostility, the emotions of stress, were largely responsible. In other words, it's all right to be a workaholic, just don't be an angry, hostile workaholic. And if you are, for heaven's sake, don't internalize it. That makes things even worse.

Let's consider now the so-called Type C personality. This is the person who is the opposite of the controller, one you would call the accommodator. This person is in a lose/win mode. "I'm going to lose; you're going to win. Your needs are more important than mine. There's no point in talking about this since we're going to do it your way, anyway."

This is the person that behavioral researcher Lydia Temoshok labeled as the Type C or cancer-prone individual. It's the person psychiatrist George Solomon described as being susceptible to rheumatoid arthritis. One who is passive and will endure a great deal of personal discomfort in order to please other people.

Evidence suggests the Type C individual has a difficult time dealing with negative emotions, especially in others. In a clinical setting, this person will wait until her throat is parched before troubling the staff for a glass of water. Then she will apologize for having taken their time.

She's just the opposite of the Type A patient who constantly is commanding the nurses' time. Demanding to know, "Why am I taking this medication, and what do you mean waking me at two o'clock in the morning to give me a sleeping pill?" It's the person who in a clinical setting is often labeled as difficult to manage. It's no surprise that's the person who does not get much extra attention. Yet, despite this, the demanding person is the one who is most likely going to survive; whereas the passive, sweet individual is likely to experience a worse outcome. Why is that?

Reflect for a moment on these two personalities, but from the standpoint of control. The person asking the questions would not do so if he did not believe he could influence the outcome. In other words, he has made himself a part of the negotiation of his treatment. In contrast, the Type C individual has essentially abdicated responsibility, handing it over to the healthcare provider: "Here I am. Do whatever you need to do."

Undoubtedly, there are likely many factors and explanations as to why one person has a better prognosis than another. But there is no question in my mind that giving up control is a very important variable. Behaving like a victim is never healthy.

There's another personality type that you hear about, which is the so-called Type T or thrill-seeking personality. These people take calculated risks and include bungee jumpers, skydivers, and motorcycle racers. This is a person who explores new horizons and is always looking for a different way to do things. It's the person who makes discoveries and who is not afraid of risk, indeed, who thrives on it.

It doesn't hurt to have at least a small amount of Type T in your makeup. That's because doing something different, even if it's positive, carries the inherent risk of failure. The unwillingness to take chances may be what's keeping you from embarking on a new endeavor. Often, fear of failure is the impediment preventing the achievement of goals.

Just like beliefs, it is not the personality that's good or bad, but the context in which it is exhibited. The same style may be detrimental under some circumstances, and beneficial under others.

Thank goodness all of our mothers were, at least temporarily, Type Cs and willing to sacrifice their own need for sleep in order to nurture us as infants. We would never have survived had they not been willing to do so. In that environment, being a Type C is a beneficial response. It is not good, however, when you are recovering in a hospital bed and place other people's needs ahead of your own. In that setting, you're the one in need of nurturing if you're to survive.

For everything, there is a season and that includes your personality. Actually, your personalities (plural), because, in fact, you are a composite of different personalities. I hope you don't interact with your children in the same way that you interact with your coworkers. I hope you don't treat your spouse in the way you treat subordinates. I hope your personality does vary depending upon the circumstance. And for that reason, I wish we could dispense with the label of personality altogether because it's really a coping style. Problems arise when an inappropriate coping style is displayed in the environment where it emerges.

When does that happen? When your beliefs give rise to mental images that fail to accurately depict reality. If you want to accomplish the things you know you can, but just don't, be aware that you need a healthy mix of several coping styles. When facing challenges in pursuit of a goal, there will be times when collaboration may either be essential or will at least smooth the way. At other times, taking control may be best. How you inter-act with others may be paramount in determining how successful you will be in achieving objectives.

Takeaways

- Perceiving you have a measure of control can help counter the impact of stress.
- When all else fails, you always have control over your attitude.
- Do nothing because you regard it as a choice, not because you feel you have no other option.
- During stressful times, your personality can sometimes become the opposite of what is normal for you.
- The negative consequences of helplessness can be counteracted if there are other pathways to closure.
- We are all composites of different personalities and temperaments. Each can be viewed as a coping style.

12

Because I'm Always Sick

et's be realistic. It doesn't matter how much motivation you might have had or the resources available to achieve a goal, nothing is going to happen while you're coping with fatigue and discomfort. These are common symptoms associated with many illnesses. That's why maintaining a state of optimal health is a prerequisite when setting about to achieve an objective.

Achieving a state of optimal health requires a robust immune system, which in turn needs three essential ingredients to keep infections at bay: healthful nutrition, exercise, and adequate sleep. This chapter will provide a brief description of the immune system, along with instructions on how to maintain it.

The cells and tissues comprising your immune system have two major jobs: (1) to keep disease-causing bugs out of your body, and (2) if those bugs do get in, destroy them. Healthy skin, mucous membranes along with the immune system defenses are located where pathogens are most likely to enter your body. They include the airways in your nose, those leading to your lungs, and those ending in the gastrointestinal system.

The immune system serves as a defense against invading microorganisms. Like any army, it needs to be fed, exercised, and kept sharp. When called into action, it attacks viruses by launching chemical cruise missiles that seek out and destroy the intruders. So what does the immune system have to do with procrastination and meeting deadlines? How about the fact the energy needed to combat an illness is energy that will not be available to achieve the tasks on your to-do list? Or how about the way the discomfort you'll experience if you develop an infection will erode whatever motivation is required to get started. Needless to say, maintaining a healthy immune system is very important.

How to Stay Healthy

You need to understand that exposure to microbes is inevitable and that steps need to be taken to reduce the likelihood that the exposure will culminate in clinical symptoms. That's why mask wearing, social distancing, and vigorous hand washing are strongly recommended by health agencies to curtail the spread of the COVID-19 virus. The immune system comes into play when these protocols fail and a virus or other pathogen enters the body. However, the immune system has to be properly maintained if it's to perform effectively. This can best be achieved through regular exercise, healthy sleep, and good nutrition.

Avoid foods and beverages that may contain drugs capable of interfering with sleep. This includes caffeine, which is found in tea, energy drinks, and coffee, as well as in many over-the-counter medications such as Excedrin and NoDoz. Many people are surprised to learn it's even found in chocolate. Caffeine triggers a hormonal cascade that's not going to help you fall asleep.

Eating moderate portions of a well-balanced diet is also paramount. The same guidelines discussed in chapter 10 need to be followed to achieve optimal immunity. In addition, it is especially important to get adequate amounts of vitamin C, which is required for wound healing as well as for normal functioning of the immune cells that wrap their membranes around invaders bringing about their destruction. Meet your nutritional needs by eating whole foods whenever you can.

If stress appears to be a factor in precipitating illness, use at least two approaches in dealing with the stress: Focus on the perception of events using cognitive techniques. If your perception that an event is threatening can be reduced, the physiological events will be as well. At the same time, feedback signals capable of potentiating cognitive events need to be reduced. Deep breathing exercises, massage, and moderate exercise can be extremely helpful.

Moderate exercise in the aerobic zone for thirty minutes three to five times each week increases the levels of an immune system chemical that stimulates T cells as well as slow-wave sleep, which is what you need to awaken in a well-rested state. It's also the stage of sleep during which growth hormone is release. As its name implies, it promotes the growth and expansion of cells including those that comprise a healthy immune system.

Take steps to prevent infection by consuming plenty of water. This can be via drinking as well as ingesting fruits and vegetables with high water content. Both the microbe-fighting skin and mucous secretions require that you remain properly hydrated in order to function optimally.

The immune system, however, does considerably more than simply protect us from disease. Do you know that some forms of depression have now been linked with the immune system? Or that chemicals produced by the immune system can affect your memory and reaction time? Even sleep and the ability to awaken feeling refreshed are linked with your immune system, yet many people harm this important healing system because of the widely advertised belief that more is always better. Like most everything in nature, a healthy balance is optimal—not too much or too little.

It's all well and good to want more immunity if you've had chemotherapy and your immune system has been derailed, or if you are highly susceptible to infections. Under these circumstances, you may very well want to take steps to boost your immune system. But if you have any type of inflammatory disease or auto-immune illness, if you suffer from severe allergies, or if you've received a transplanted organ, the last thing you may want to do is try to boost your immune system. In fact, you may want to take steps to bring down your immune system, not to enhance it. That's how transplants are managed and some allergies are controlled.

Your immune system is a double-edged sword. You don't want less, which will leave you susceptible to infections, but neither do you want too much. You need immunologic balance.

Eat Less

Here's a nutritional option I strongly recommend. It will enhance the immune system when it's too low, it'll bring it down when it's too high, and it seems to have the wisdom to know what is required. The intervention is eat less. The renowned immunologist Robert Good showed reducing caloric intake can alleviate the symptoms of those susceptible to infections, as well as of those who are prone to autoimmunity.

Eating less will not make the diseases disappear. Instead, it renders the symptoms more manageable. It's not clear how this works, although many scientists believe the benefits are due to reducing oxidative-metabolites also known as free radicals, a natural by-product of oxidative metabolism. Excess production of these chemicals has been linked with a large number of chronic illnesses, so reducing their number would logically be associated with improved overall health.

There are various ways to reduce calorie intake. In the laboratory, researchers will determine how much freely available food is consumed over a twenty-four-hour interval by test animals. That amount is defined as the free-feeding diet. It's essentially the amount of food the animal wants. Then it's reduced to between 80 and 90 percent of that desired amount.

We aren't lab rats, but some people will follow a similar approach by counting calories, while others engage in intermittent fasting. They intersperse days without food with those when it's consumed. There are different ways to achieve the same end, but the research arrives at the same conclusion. Reducing caloric intake can be a key feature of a healthy lifestyle.

Here's an easy way for you to take advantage of this information. Eat as much food as you need. Eat it whenever you want, but when you reach the point when you don't need any more, but you still may want seconds or thirds, push your plate away. You'll leave the table feeling just a little bit hungry, but you know you'll be fine.

Next, eat dessert. That is important for three reasons. First, when you know dessert is coming, it's easier to push the entrée plate away. Not only that, but it takes time to clear away the entrée and bring dessert to the table. During that time, there's a period when the chemical messages from your stomach can get to your brain, signaling that you are full. A lot of people eat too quickly so by the time the "I'm full" signal arrives in the brain, it's too late. You may already have consumed perhaps 20 percent more food that you not only did not need, but that you also did not even want.

Recognize, too, that dessert brings closure to the meal. It's the official end, and when you have that taste of the sweet flavor in your mouth, you are less inclined to rip another piece of flesh off the chicken carcass sitting on the counter. No, I'm not suggesting that you gorge on ice cream. You can have fresh fruit. Dessert might consist of tea or coffee. It doesn't matter how you do it, as long as it's a ritual that brings closure to the meal.

Prevention Is Better Than a Cure

Nothing will interfere more with your pleasure and productivity than an infection. Here are some steps that translate the information described thus far into practical ways to decrease the probability of contracting an infection and, if you do get one, to experience a speedier recovery. Prevention, prevention, prevention. Without question, take steps to avoid exposure to cold-causing viruses. That includes keeping your nose clean. Literally.

Keep your hands away from your face. Rhinovirus, one of the more common viruses that causes common cold symptoms, has got to get deep into the nasopharynx in order to trigger symptoms. This region is where the nasal passages and oral cavity join. From there, it has easy access to the lungs. Unless it gets in there, it's not going to make you sick.

Begin by keeping your hands away from your nose and your eyes. On average, most people's hands wander up to their eyes or noses at least once each minute, often more than that. If you simply train yourself to curtail this unhealthy habit, you will decrease the probability of developing an infection.

Keep your hands clean. Wash your hands, especially when you're around other people who are sick. Shaking hands or touching the same surfaces that they have definitely will increase your chances of picking up a virus and developing a cold or flu. And move away from people who are sneezing or coughing. Many viruses are aerosols, which means they are transmitted through the air thereby infecting innocent bystanders.

There is no question that when people with colds or flu take precautions by simply covering their noses and mouths before coughing and sneezing, they significantly reduce the probability of transmitting that virus to someone else. As the coronavirus is spreading throughout the world, the wearing of masks not only reduces the transmission of that virus, but also those viruses that cause the common cold and influenza. The masks have proven highly effective in preventing the incidence of a number of viral illnesses.

Make sure you have plenty of vitamin C in your diet. While there's limited evidence extra vitamin C can prevent a cold, that's only in people subjected to extra demands on their immune system. There is no question adequate (the amount recommended by the FDA) vitamin C in your diet is necessary to maintain a healthy immune system. But keep the amount in the 70 to 90 mg range, which is recommended by the Academy of Nutrition and Dietetics. That's because excessive amounts in the form of supplements can cause problems.

Keep your hands to yourself. Avoid surfaces where viruses may lurk. A cold virus may be able to survive for up to several hours after landing on a surface. Be careful when in fitness centers. People who are working out and perspiring are constantly wiping their faces and spreading viruses if they happen to be recovering from a cold. When they place their sweaty palms on the handholds of a treadmill or on free weights, they are transferring that virus to the surface you may later touch. I'm not saying to stop working out. Just take extra precautions if you work out during flu season by paying attention to those who used the equipment before you.

Your immune system is your best weapon against viral infections. Don't waste your time or money taking antibiotics. All they'll do is destroy the good bacteria that reside in your GI system, resulting in stomach upset. Save antibiotics for what they are designed for: destroying the bacteria capable of causing harm.

The best things to do are drink lots of fluids and follow your body's cues to get plenty of bed rest. It's during slow-wave sleep that growth hormone is released, and that is a very powerful pick-me-up for your immune system. Go to bed an hour earlier than usual, and you'll get an extra dose of that healing sleep.

Eat chicken soup. It works, especially if it's hot. A lot of microbes cannot survive higher than normal temperatures, so when that hot soup passes down your throat, you are creating a very inhospitable environment for pathogens that happen to be lurking there.

Furthermore, chicken, like most foods that contain protein, has an amino acid called cystine. This is released from the meat when the soup is prepared. It so happens there is a striking biochemical similarity between cystine and a drug called acetylcysteine, which is precisely what doctors prescribe for those people who have bronchitis and respiratory infections.

Indeed, acetylcysteine was originally extracted from chicken feathers and skin. It thins the mucus in the lungs facilitating its expulsion, which, of course, is going to take trapped viruses with it. Add some hot peppers and spice, and you'll increase the beneficial effects. That's because peppers and hot curry powders can stimulate salivation. This also helps to thin the virus-laden mucus, making it easier to expel. And don't forget to add a little garlic, which has natural antimicrobial properties.

Take care of those around you. Even though your foremost concern might be eliminating your own symptoms, you need to make sure your significant other does not get sick, or else he or she may not be able to prepare that hot soup or run down to the market to get the medications you need.

Colds are most infectious during the first three days after the first symptoms appear. That's when you are transmitting a maximum number of viruses into the environment. By the fourth day, your risk to others is significantly reduced, even though you may still be experiencing symptoms. In fact, it probably will take a full two weeks to eliminate all the vestiges of a cold, but it's during that first three-day period when you are most contagious.

Stay upbeat. Research conducted at Carnegie Mellon University has found that the more positive you are, the less likely you are to catch a cold in the first place. After you do experience symptoms, they will be less severe than those in people who lack a positive attitude. Rent humorous videos or read an upbeat novel. Talk to a friend—on the phone, of course, until you've passed through the most infectious stage. Social support does wonders for your health.

Eliminate dairy products if you have a cold. The protein in cow's milk can irritate the immune system of some people. Furthermore, milk products are also more likely to increase mucus production, which will increase congestion.

Allow a fever to run its course as long as it is not excessive. Many pathogens cannot survive when body temperature goes up even a few degrees.

Make a steam tent by placing a towel over a pot of hot water and inhale the steam for a period of ten minutes. Remember, microbes don't like high temperatures.

Add a quarter teaspoon of salt to one cup of warm water and gargle at least once every half hour until the symptoms of the sore throat begin to abate. The heat will agitate the virus, and the salt will disrupt its membrane.

Expectations, Beliefs, and Immunity

Let's now consider how beliefs can influence your health. Placebos represent the most convincing line of evidence there is a link between the mind and the body. A placebo is a drug, for example, that you take to bring about a cure, but let's say you don't know that there are no active ingredients in the pill you take. Low and behold, you get better just like the person who got the real medicine.

What is known as the placebo effect (the cure) is triggered by your beliefs and expectations. Pharmaceutical companies are well aware of this, which is the reason various colors, tastes, and textures are used when marketing drugs—to take advantage of its potential.

Imagine you have never heard of an herbal remedy recently introduced to the US market. Experts claim, "This product, if taken according to our instructions, will cure your arthritis, multiple sclerosis, allergies, and keep you from catching colds and flu." Elsewhere in the brochure are personal testimonials from patients and claims by doctors.

How is this advertised claim likely to influence you? If you're a skeptic, then your response might wisely be, "This is too good to be true." On the other hand, the image created by these words may increase your expectations that the product will do the same for you. Obviously, there are ethical considerations when advising a person to take a placebo. However, this phenomenon provides further evidence of just how powerful a person's beliefs can be in shifting the often delicate balance between good health and disease.

I overheard while taking a break from a lecture tour one of the most honest assessments of how remedies work from a homeopath in London. While looking around her store, an agitated lady marched to the counter, reached in her shopping bag and placed a half-empty vial of medicine onto the counter. She loudly declared, "This medicine has not helped my arthritis at all. In fact, I knew it wasn't going to help when I bought it. It may have made my arthritis even worse, so I would like my money back, please."

The shopkeeper responded by saying, "Mrs. Jones, with that attitude, I'm not surprised the medicine didn't work. It's a homeopathic medicine. It can't work by itself. You have to help it by changing your attitude. Now take what's left of this medicine and think positively about it. Believe in it, and then if it still doesn't work, I will give you your money back."

Mrs. Jones got very flustered. She said, "Yes, of course, you're right. I'll try that," and off she went.

That was the essence of the conversation I couldn't help overhearing. How I wish I could have recorded that exchange because that homeopath was being honest. She was acknowledging what everyone who dispenses any type of medicine should. Nothing is working for a single reason.

One of the most enduring pathways to optimal health is lined with your beliefs. Use them to achieve your health goals in the same way you can attain other types of goals.

Is It Right for You?

One size never has nor ever will fit all, and that applies to some of the recommendations described in this chapter. In some instances, especially when dealing with choices pertaining to health, the appropriate answer to "why don't I" might be "because I shouldn't do it!" We are constantly being subjected to advertised, cultural, or hand-me-down beliefs that sound good, but there's always that nagging question, "Is it right for me?" A darned good question because what may be a perfect solution for one person may be a disaster for another.

This is particularly true of medical claims, which should always be supported with data. If the FDA proclaims that an effect is significant after all the proper tests, we have a tendency to embrace the belief that the protocol will do the same for us. It's not that simple. Nothing pertaining to health is.

First, what the statistics assume is that everyone who participated in the study is basically the same. In other words, subjects are chosen because they match similar criteria such as a specific age or gender. Then, if the majority of those selected respond in the desired way, scientists conclude the intervention is effective.

But what if you are not average? What if you are a part of the minority for whom the protocol may be harmful or a part of the smaller group likely to experience the listed side effects?

Let's consider the opposite scenario whereby an intervention is rejected because the majority of those in a study failed to experience a beneficial effect. Could you be a person for whom the protocol might be just what you need to improve your health and well-being? And what about available options, but because they are not regulated don't have to be tested? How can you tell if those are avenues you should be trying? It's not easy to answer these questions because many variables influence health. Nonetheless, there is some information you should be armed with so that you can at least make an informed decision.

Collect Pertinent Data

You'll begin by doing some background research. In this case, it's about yourself, and what better place to start than with your relatives. That's because you have their genes, which served as the architectural plans used to construct your body. If you inherited a gene predisposing you to a specific malady, there may be steps you can take to reduce the likelihood of experiencing the same fate.

For example, if heart disease runs in your family, adopt the DASH (Dietary Approaches to Stop Hypertension) program. Its primary recommendation is a diet low in saturated fat and cholesterol and high in fruits and vegetables. There are other dietary guidelines as well, which have been shown to reduce blood pressure and reduce the risk of heart disease. The risk of some cancers and Type 2 diabetes also can be attenuated through the use of exercise and diet.

Evaluating Medical Claims

From now on, whenever you are presented with an advertised belief promoting a new and improved version of dietary advice, you will have the definitive test at your disposal. But before you begin, you'll need a heart rate monitor, a watch, and access to either a bicycle ergometer or treadmill with an odometer attached. Actually, you could use any exercise for this test. I recommend stationary fitness equipment because it's easier to be consistent.

The procedure will always be the same. Warm up until your heart rate reaches approximately 75 percent of your maximum. Your maximum heart rate is best determined by an exercise physiologist in a controlled setting; however, you can approximate the value by subtracting your age from 220 (220 minus your age). If you are forty, your maximum would be 220–40 or 180 beats per minute. And then 75 percent of this value would be 135 beats per minute as your maximum heart rate.

Next, note the time and keep your heart rate as close to that level as you can for exactly five minutes. You are going to measure two variables: (1) the distance traveled during the five-minute test, and (2) the time it takes for your heart rate to return to 50 percent of your maximum. For a person whose age is forty, it would be 220–40 = 180 x 0.50 or 90 beats per minute. Make every attempt to keep the conditions exactly the same each time you do this. This is especially important with respect to the warm-up and cool-down phase of the regimen.

You now have a protocol you can use to evaluate whatever you're considering as a way to improve your overall health. Granted, there may be more relevant systems to assess for some health issues, but assessing the cardiovascular system based upon heart rate recovery is easy, noninvasive, and costs nothing. Every organ in your body depends on the oxygen and nutrients delivered in blood so heart function is a pretty good place to start.

In addition, the ability of your heart rate to recover quickly after the stress of exercise is a good predictor of how quickly the rest of your body will recover from other forms of stress over which you have limited control. Keep in mind that stress is like a stone thrown into a pond. It doesn't take long for the ripples to travel throughout a body of water. Stress similarly ripples throughout your body where it can interfere with a wide range of activities including sleep, memory, and mood along with many others.

Begin by completing the heart-rate-based protocol before trying whatever you have chosen to improve your well-being. It's a five-minute routine at the 75 percent level followed by a brief interval until your heart rate drops to 50 percent. Your chosen intervention might be a supplement proclaimed to improve sleep, or a pill being advertised to expand your memory, or some concoction advertised to reduce your anxiety. After you have established your baseline values of time to reach a heart rate of 50 percent and distance traveled, repeat the protocol and compare the values before and after the intervention you're evaluating.

As a result of consuming health-promoting foods or supplements, your entire body should function at a greater level of efficiency, including the ability of your heart rate to recover. That means at the same heart rate, you will be able to cover a greater distance and your heart rate will recover faster.

Remember, exercise is a form of physical stress. Consequently, you are testing the effects of the intervention on your ability to perform under stress. What works during exercise also will serve you well when dealing with conflict in the office, negotiating with your teenager, or dealing with the myriad of daily stressors that are simply unavoidable.

No, the test is not perfect. Each time you do this brief workout, there will be a modest training effect (you'll do better just because you were doing the exercise). It's also important to perform the pre- and post-routine close to the same time of day to minimize the influence of daily fluctuations in hormones that might influence the outcome.

You can use a similar process to evaluate other claims. For example, establish a scale from 1 to 10 for whatever it is you want to improve. Sleep, perhaps? Then establish 1 as the equivalent of awakening in a coma and 10 with wanting to complete an ultra-marathon. The other numbers would be correlated with intermediate states. Keep score each morning for at least a week prior to starting the new intervention. Then, put your notes out of sight in a drawer and start a new page.

For the next week, continue keeping score while continuing with the purported sleeping remedy. Compare the results with those recorded during the first week. Was there an improvement with no side effects? Then keep doing it. No change? Then save your money or try something else.

You can use this protocol to evaluate virtually anything that you want to improve: memory, endurance, mood, motivation, or libido. Just because you saw the commercial on TV or read about it on the internet doesn't mean the remedy will work for you in the same way or at all.

It's your body, and it's different from everyone else's. Be skeptical of any protocol being promoted as a solution. It's highly unlikely that what would be suitable for a sedentary, middle-aged man with diabetes would be appropriate for a woman who is a triathlete. Of course your body changes over time, so what works in the summer may not be effective in the winter. Always confirm a remedy is right for you before embracing it.

Takeaways

- The immune system is multifaceted with cells, chemicals, and physical barriers comprising it.
- Every component of the immune system can benefit from healthful nutrition, exercise, and sleep.

- Eating what you need instead of what you want can improve your immune system.
- Prevention of illness is always the best way to achieve optimal health.
- Effective management of stress also helps prevent illness.
- Question the interpretation of data, then confirm a remedy is effective in meeting your needs before committing.

So What's Your Excuse?

Congratulations! You've arrived at the end of this book and have discovered the answer to "why don't you do it?" Too emotional? A born procrastinator? Afraid of failure? Maybe you think you can't do anything right, especially when you have no one you can lean on for support.

If these and the other excuses discussed don't resonate with you, perhaps none of the more common reasons apply to you. That's to be expected since one size doesn't fit all. No matter, you now know why you do what you do and, with that understanding, how best to change your ways. Another option is to do what I did.

Instead of changing my ways, I chose jobs that provided a source of the excitement I found rewarding. Wrestling alligators, milking rattlesnakes, toiling from grant to grant as a scientist knowing my source of income could dry up if the next series of experiments didn't pan out. A stint with the US intelligence community, then walking away from academia to try my hand in the competitive world of corporate America. For recreation, I ride my bicycle thousands of miles across the US. Changing the environment is an option we all have.

Procrastination doesn't need to be in your vocabulary any longer. When you learn to manage your emotions, you can manage most any task you are qualified to perform. You no longer need to be afraid you'll fail. Maybe you will fail. So what? Heed the wisdom of T. S. Eliot who recognized that "Only those who will risk going too far can possibly find out how far one can go."

Did you recognize any of the beliefs described in this book to be personal obstacles to attaining goals? If so, stop allowing them to hold you back any longer. Some of those beliefs may need to be shown the door, in which case use this book to hold it open.

I'll admit we don't always know what we want in life, never mind what we want at the grocery store. But it's time to make some decisions and figure out where we're going and how to get there.

None of us can accomplish everything we desire if we try to go it alone. Even though I ride solo across the country on my bike, I'm never really alone. All along the way, I'm met with acts of kindness at truck stops, parks, and even along lonely stretches of highway where strangers will ask if I need water or other supplies. Yours is a different type of journey, yet you can still seek those who will support your efforts while distancing yourself from those who won't.

If you find yourself saying you never have enough time, or do anything right, think again. Everything you do can make a difference for you or for someone else. But don't overlook your personal needs. Take care of your own emotional and physical health by seeking the right balance between work and family. Prevention is always better than a cure.

I have presented health-related information at continuing medical education seminars to thousands of people across the country. Indeed, it was an audience member, Geneele Crump, who inspired the title of this book. It is my sincere hope that you have found some nuggets of advice making it possible for you to never again have to ask, *I know what to do, so why don't I do it?*

Come to think of it, by finishing this book, you've already turned over a new leaf. You did it! Now keep it up so you can enjoy the full and healthy life you so richly deserve.

Acknowledgments

I'm deeply indebted to my loving wife, Hazel, who has supported and encouraged me throughout my often zany undertakings and adventures that have provided many of the insights discussed in this book. Also, to my children and grandchildren whose rapid passage through their life cycles has taught me life is short and to seize every opportunity to relish the joys of parenthood and grandparenthood.

About the Author

Nick Hall, PhD, is a medical scientist and the recipient of an honorary medical degree from St. Georges University School of Medicine and who since 1979 has conducted groundbreaking studies linking the mind and body. His psychoneuroimmunology research has been featured on CBS *60 Minutes*, the BBC's Nova series, and the Emmy Award–winning television program *Healing and the Mind* produced by Bill Moyers for PBS.

In addition to his academic pursuits, Nick is no stranger to the more pragmatic aspects of how emotions impact health and performance. After earning his way through college wrestling alligators and milking rattlesnakes at the Black Hills Reptile Gardens in South Dakota, he spent two years training whales and dolphins as part of an Office of Naval Research project to decipher stress-related communication patterns in dolphins.

This was followed by an expedition sponsored by the National Geographic Society to the West Indies where he studied mass-stranding behavior in whales. He's also worked as an intelligence-operative for the US government and taught at the FBI National Academy in Quantico, Virginia.

Since 2015, he has traveled more than 10,000 miles bicycling alone across the United States to raise awareness and money to support Rotary International's effort to eradicate polio.

He currently directs the Wellness Center at Saddlebrook Resort near Tampa, Florida, where he conducts workshops and team-building programs for corporate clients and athletes.

CPSIA information can be obtained
at www.ICGtesting.com
Printed in the USA
JSHW031131140222
PP11441900001B/1

9 781722 505707